Mein erster
Schultag
DEMENAGEZ AVEC
RYDER

Identity

From Holocaust to Home

A MEMOIR

ELKE BABICKI

THE HISTORY COLLECTIVES

THE HISTORY
COLLECTIVES

Elke Babicki

Identity: From Holocaust to Home

The History Collectives

First Edition

Print ISBN 978-1-7775039-0-1

Cover & Book Design | Kristy Hill, Umbrella Squared Design Group

Originally published by Verlag Attenkofer , Germany

Dedicated to:
My Family

Contents

Preface

Some of my Canadian friends who have known me for decades seem convinced that my life only began once I arrived in Canada. They are not completely wrong.

They are not completely right, either. I always had a feeling that it was not the right moment to share my stories. Who wants to hear about Alex, my Polish Jewish father, who survived by hiding beneath dead bodies in a concentration camp? Does someone really want to hear how my German grandfather, Johann, was taken from his wife and small children by the SS and carried off to the concentration camp in Dachau? I didn't think so.

As time has passed, however, I've come to see telling my family's story as essential. The suffering that the National Socialists brought to the people—to Jews, to German men at the front, to women alone at home, and to children who grew up without fathers—is pain that has passed on through generations. Yet, the courage of men and women who struggled to survive, the true stories can never be shut down or killed. Their survival has meaning and telling their story is the one thing I can do to contribute to it not happening ever again.

The unaccountably powerful set out to destroy my family's lives, which resulted in a life filled with hardship and post-traumatic stress disorders for my entire family. But they did what they could to rally to new expectations. Their ability to overcome taught me to persevere, to draw strength, to show courage, to be daring, to look forward, to listen to my intuition and gut instinct and to trust carefully chosen people.

My parents and grandparents taught me how important it is to pay attention, especially to our inner guidance—and even take certain dreams seriously. They can lead us to safety, where I am today—on the other side of the Atlantic Ocean from the world of my childhood.

This book is based on my family's stories, experiences and memories and is largely as accurate as stories and memories can be. However, I have changed some names. There are also characters in this book who are entirely fictional, to allow me to describe something that happened with sufficient detail and intensity. All of the main characters represent members of my actual family.

PART ONE

Chapter 1

New life, old wounds—and a stubborn kind of hope

Tilly and Alex, Straubing, Germany, early 1950s

THE SCISSORS SLIPPED FROM TILLY'S HAND AS SHE OPENED the last carton of pickles, bounced off the tile counter, hit the floor and slid under a small wooden shelf. She knelt down and reached into the dark space.

As she ran her hand across the floor under the shelf, she felt a bundle of letters pushed all the way back against the wall. She would never have noticed it just looking at the shelf from above, the way she usually did.

Tilly reached for the bundle. There were at least twelve envelopes bound with a string. The ones on the bottom were already more yellow and tattered. But they all looked as if they'd been torn open hastily, without using a letter opener.

He had pulled these letters out many times and always pushed them back again, of that she was sure. She brushed her index finger across the top envelope, the cord, the stamps and the red cross printed over the top.

So, he hides them here—in the shop rather than our home, she thought, and sighed softly. She would have liked to read those letters. But now she had no time. She had to continue her preparations for opening the store. In just a few minutes, the first customers would arrive.

Tilly slid the envelopes back into their hiding spot, then retrieved the scissors. She stood up and bent to take two glass jars of pickles from the carton she had been working on. She placed them on the counter beside the scale. She had already wiped the board in the shop's display case and decorated it with red-and-white-checkered napkins. Now, she added the pickle jars, always with the labels facing forward, in a neat row. She bent again and placed three jars of mustard, two jars of beets and two containers of pickled celery into the display.

She wiped her hands on the apron and grabbed the empty carton, squeezing it so she wouldn't accidently knock anything down in the narrow space behind the counter. Then she went to check the display.

Behind the glass Tilly had cleaned a few hours ago sat a large baked ham, a Black Forest ham, smoked raw *bauernschinken*, smoked salami, sliced salami, a platter of bratwurst, a whole mountain of white sausages, and more than ten pairs of wieners. She had decorated the display with lettuce leaves, radishes and tomatoes. In front of the turkey breast, beef tenderloin and veal cutlets, she had placed small handwritten signs so that the customers could see the prices. In between, the steel plate they'd polished the evening before gleamed. On the tiled walls of the store behind the display counter dangled various types of salami, Polish sausage and liverwurst. Tilly had tied the knots in the threads at the end of each sausage so she could attach them to one of the many hooks.

She smiled contentedly and dried her face with a handkerchief. Strands of her light brown hair stuck to her temples. She had been working to stock the sausage and meat counter since the early morning, but now it was time to get herself together. She went into the adjoining private room, which functioned as a kitchen and dining room, with a couch to relax on. She put the carton aside and scrubbed her hands with soap in the sink.

She went to the couch and retrieved her make-up bag from the shelf beside it, snapping it open to pull out her little folding mirror.

Tilly brushed her fingers over her dark eyebrows, drew a narrow stroke of eyeliner at the edge of each lid and dabbed a little blush on her cheeks. She combed her shoulder-length hair back, and, finally, carefully applied a delicate rose-colored lipstick. One last look in the mirror to check that there were no smears on her teeth—all fine. She took off her work apron and put it aside on the kitchen chair for the laundry later. Reaching into the shelf for her freshly laundered white coat, she buttoned it over her dress. She slipped from her flat brown shoes into finer blue shoes with heels before returning to the store.

Behind the counter, she sorted the notes and coins into the right slots in the cash register. She filled the candy jar with bonbons, their silver-colored wrappers rustling as they tumbled into the jar.

It reminded her of her childhood. There were more treats in her hand now than all the candies she'd eaten during her childhood combined. Once, Tilly had had a girlfriend who sometimes brought one or even two candies from home. Walking along the Danube, they had carefully unwrapped them on the way to school and tried to suck them as slowly as possible. Tilly had kept the glittering papers in her skirt pocket for weeks to look at them again and again.

Now, the container was filled to the brim with sweets, and she slipped the lid over it.

"Tilly," she heard her husband, Alex, call.

"I'm here."

There was a loud whrrmm as he pushed open the sliding door of his van.

Tilly had left the back door open so she could hear his arrival. She went into the yard where the van was parked. Alex was already rushing towards the other side of the courtyard and had opened the door to the cold store.

"Wait, Alex, I'll help you unload," she said.

Alex, a few inches taller than her and very slender, also wore a white work coat over his white shirt and black trousers. A dark blue tie with little white dots completed his carefully chosen outfit.

Now he hurried into the cold store and switched on the light. Tilly went to the van, lifted a crate and carried it across the yard to him. Coming out of the cold store, he smiled, kissed her on the cheek and took the crate from her. They worked until the van was empty.

"We should have enough meat here for today," Alex said. "But I definitely have to check on the sausage production." Whenever he said something or smiled, the edge of a golden tooth in the upper row of his teeth flashed in the sun.

He pushed the side door of the van shut and opened the driver's door. He took out a letter and tucked it under his arm. Tilly immediately recognized the red cross on the envelope. Alex had received another reply.

As they went into the shop together, Alex combed his hair to the side and smoothed it with his hand. Tilly gently straightened his necktie and brushed her hand over his sleeve where she had spotted a piece of lint.

"Have you already opened it?" she asked.

He took the letter from under his arm and she saw he had torn it open.

"And?" she asked again, stroking his upper arm.

"No," he said, looking at the tiled floor and shaking his head. "Nothing."

For five years, Alex had been writing to the Red Cross. He asked questions, filled out forms, carefully spelled out his family name, Michalowicz, just in case it had been missed the previous time. When finally a response came in the mail, it seemed the tension was intolerable to him. And the disappointment was getting worse each time he learned that nothing about his family had been found.

He put the letter on the small shelf under the counter but did not push it to the back where Tilly had discovered the hidden bundle. For a moment, he stood quietly, his lips pressed together tightly.

"So nice, how you decorated everything," he said. He regarded the display, trying to smile.

"This is my domain, and this is how I like it," she said, returning the smile.

Tilly and Alex had previously operated another shop, located in the Albrechtsgasse in the middle of Straubing's inner city. For the first few months, they had slept on straw mattresses on the stone floor. Soon, the business was so successful they were able to open a bigger shop in the Schlesische Street in the east of the city. In this new, post-war area of the city, their shop was the first, with no competition.

After a short time, they had the new shop running well, and they had furnished a little apartment above it.

Alex was a born businessman. After the war, he came to Straubing and lived by trading on the black market, selling butter, sugar and cigarettes. Since he was honest and forthright, people quickly trusted and depended on him. After only a few months, he had built a considerable network and established contacts with important people in town.

Among the Straubing townspeople who had helped Alex was Johann, who worked to help Jews find a place to stay and make business contacts in the city.

One day, Alex had wanted to thank Johann and brought a kilo of sugar to his house on Gstütt Island. Instead of Johann, a pretty young girl, seventeen-year-old Ottilie, opened the door. Her brown eyes solemnly appraised the visitor.

"Father," she had yelled, "there is somebody here to see you."

Alex didn't know then that they would be married and open their first shop a few years later. Ottilie had worked in a grocery store in the city during the war, learning the trade of a saleswoman during a time when there was almost nothing to sell.

The two learned to rely on each other—their mutual trust was a rare commodity they both cherished above all else.

"Now," Alex said, "I'll just check on the sausage production." He disappeared from the shop.

He needs time to think about the letter, Tilly knew. That was always the case when a Red Cross response arrived.

She took the last letter from the shelf and unfolded the page. "Dear Mr. Michalowicz—With regret, we write to inform you ..."

The rest of the typewritten message stated that, at this time, there was no information about the whereabouts of Alex's three sisters, two brothers, mother and father.

"Not even one. They can't even find one," Tilly whispered to herself.

The uncertainty reminded her of when her family hadn't known whether her fifteen-year-old brother, Hans, was dead or alive at the end of the war. They had heard only that he had fallen into Russian hands as a prisoner of war. For three years, they had no news. In 1948, fortunately, the Russians released another prisoner who was from Straubing. He knew Tilly's parents and came to their home to tell them that Hans was still alive—that they had worked together in a mine. After that, they at least had hope again.

Tilly was startled out of her reverie when the little bell above the entrance door chimed. Normally the large glass windows gave her advance notice of anyone approaching the store, but this time she hadn't seen anyone coming.

As she straightened, she saw her father, Johann, clinging to the door frame with one hand, pale and out of breath.

"Father, what's the matter?" she cried, rushing out from behind the counter.

"Ottilie," he stammered, looking at her with wide eyes.

"Father, please be calm. Breathe, breathe deeply."

Sweat ran down her father's face, and Tilly put her hand on his forehead to check for a fever. But his temperature felt normal.

Even the distance from Gstütt to here is a real struggle for him now, she thought. Her father had to be careful because his lungs had not properly healed since he was shot in the war. Again and again, his stomach bled and the shoulder through which he was shot gave him constant trouble.

"Sit down. I'll get you a cup of water," she said. Tilly opened a little folding chair that she always had ready for older customers and pushed him into it. "Stay and rest," she urged, before rushing to get him a glass of water. "Papa, drink," Tilly held the cup to his lips. She saw that the elongated scar above his left cheek had healed well and the many small scars on his neck were visible only under close scrutiny.

He took a sip and looked at her. "Ottilie, they're letting your brother out."

"What? What did you say?"

"We got a letter in the mail. In a few days, our boy will be home again."

As he smiled, tears filled the creases around his eyes and then ran down his weathered cheeks. His shoulders shook.

Tilly embraced her father, holding him as tightly as she could. She stroked his grey hair and began to sob. Finally, after five years, her brother would return.

When Hans didn't come home after the war, the family worried they would never see him again. Tilly watched the streets through the shop windows each day, looking for her brother among the people passing by. Would her brother carry such a bag? Had his walk changed? Each time, young men turned around to reveal features that were not her brother's.

But Tilly did not let herself be discouraged. At some point, she was sure that Hans would pass her on the street or open the door and stand before her. And now, five years later, this would really happen. She held her father closely before letting him go.

"Alex, Alex," she shouted. After a few moments, Alex came running.

"What is it? What happened?" he asked.

"Hans is coming home," Tilly whispered.

"That's unbelievable," said Alex, who had never met Tilly's brother.

Tilly could only guess what Hans had been through. Customers had told her what they knew about the Russian camps, what had happened to their husbands, brothers and sons. Sometimes, she read something about the camps in the newspaper or overheard people talking about them in the town square. The accounts were not encouraging—they spoke of torture, harassment, disease and starvation.

Yet hope won out in the shop in the Schlesische Street, where, surrounded by sausages and ham, Tilly and Alex held Johann's hands, overwhelmed by the news that Hans was coming home.

Chapter 2

Little red flags fluttering in the winds of change

Johann

Gstütt, a neighborhood in Straubing, 1937

IT WAS ONE OF THOSE DREAMS THAT STARTLED JOHANN OUT of a sound sleep. A shudder went through his upper body all the way to his fingertips. He gasped for air as if he had not been able to breathe for some time, as if something had cut off his oxygen supply. He forced his eyes to open. Cold sweat clung to his neck and his chest and his mouth felt dry. Still hazy, he turned his head to the other side of the pillow.

There, the cotton pillowcase was dry and cooled his face. By the pale light of the moon, he could make out the dark hair and smooth shoulders of his wife, Maria. She had pushed the bedcovers down to her hips and was breathing gently in deep sleep.

"It was only a dream," Johann mumbled to himself, swallowing in an attempt to moisten his dry mouth. "Just a dream."

He rested the back of his hand on his forehead—no, he didn't have a fever. Carefully, he wiped off the beads of sweat and took a deep breath. He must have been holding his breath in his sleep, because each inhalation now felt like something stabbing his lungs.

In his dream, Johann had stood across from his old friend Peter, who was often on his mind lately.

When they were young boys, Peter had been his best friend. Together, they played marbles, searched the shores of the Danube for treasures, skipped school and pulled girls' braids. They balanced on the broken ice of the Danube river close to the medieval castle and patted the farmers' horses in the Theresienplatz market square.

Then, Johann had waited with excitement for Peter to come to his home and pick him up.

These days, everything had changed.

How could it be that Peter supported Hitler? How could Peter stand in front of him, laugh in his face and say how good it was that someone was finally following through? Peter also knew Jewish people—he had to know that it was wrong to make and hang signs saying, "Jews are not welcome here." He had to know it was wrong to rob the shop of a Jewish owner without being punished. How could a mob not be punished for chasing a Jewish family with a small child from their home, never to be seen again? Wasn't it Peter who'd always said you needed to fight against evil? How could he forget all that?

But Peter was not alone.

Johann was Catholic and German. His family had lived in Straubing for generations and had always been an integral part of this tightknit community. But now he wondered if he was the only one who thought the red flags flying in the wind on the houses close to the city square did not bode well. Or the young brats who couldn't even read or write yet, but threw stones into Jewish shops and screamed the slogans of their parents, laughing when they were challenged. Was he the only one who felt threatened when they marched to the city tower, drumming and chanting while someone led with a raised index finger, yelling into a microphone? There had to be others who didn't find the dark uniforms and grim faces appealing, who didn't feel proud of the swastika armbands.

The next morning, Johann was greeted by the sun shining into their small room, and his dark thoughts from the night before had almost disappeared. He felt fortunate, at thirty-one, to have such a dear wife and children.

Maria had already gotten up to brew coffee and warm milk for Erwin, the little one. When Johann joined them in the kitchen, he found nine-year-old Ottilie kneeling on the floor, stuffing a few books and an apple into her school backpack. Hans, two years younger, observed his sister's every move.

Johann wondered, What is he up to this time? He had to grin.

On the wooden bench, Maria held Erwin on her lap. While she gave him his bottle, she hummed to herself and gently rocked back and forth.

"Do you have to go into town today?" she asked.

"Yes, Maier needs a new wooden bench for his kitchen. I have to look into that," he said, hoping that his answer would satisfy her. He quickly turned away and poured himself a cup of steaming coffee from the pot.

Maria stopped humming. She placed the bottle on the table and pointed at him. "Johann, you have to be careful." At the change in her mood, Erwin began kicking his feet. Fat tears rolled down his cheeks.

"I understand what you're doing," Maria added. "But you have to be very careful."

Erwin started screaming, his face turning red.

The tone of Maria's voice grew more urgent. "Johann, I think you are doing the right thing. But what will happen to us if they catch you?"

That was exactly the question he had been trying to avoid for a while now. Maybe this was also the question that didn't let him think clearly in the daytime or sleep soundly at night. It almost made him furious that Maria would dare to ask such a question, but when he turned toward her, he saw tears in her eyes. She held the baby against her and gently stroked his back while he whimpered and gasped for air.

"Maria," Johann said quietly, placing the cup on the table. He knelt in front of her and took her hand. "Maria, I promise you I will be careful," he assured her, pressing her hand tightly. "Trust me, please."

But Maria had closed her eyes and refused to open them, as if she refused to watch him leave the house.

As Johann walked from Gstütt Island along the river towards the town, the sunshine sparkled on the water just as it had when he'd scrambled through the bushes as a boy with Peter. The large rocks by the shore were covered with snow and the branches of the bushes bent under its weight. Chunks of ice floated along with the current. The sky was a brilliant blue, not a cloud in sight, with nothing to soften the icy cold.

Johann was thinking of Peter when he heard the laughter of children from the other shore. He stopped and watched a couple of young boys throw rocks into the water and then rub snow into each other's faces, giggling and screeching. They were maybe ten years old and wore thick fleece jackets and hats. Were they just like the other children in brown shirts, marching in the city square on Sundays? Did they believe that things would go on as before—that they would continue to play on the shores of the Danube and then sit with their mothers and fathers at the table to eat dinner? Did they stop to wonder why the Jewish girl was no longer in their classroom or why the Jewish boy was not coming to play ball? He would have liked to ask them, but he had to keep going. Maier was already waiting.

Johann hurried across the castle bridge, but then he stopped for a moment and looked at the boys. His gaze traveled along the windows of the castle, with their red and white shutters, to the large fresco depicting St. Christopher. How did the story go again? The patron saint carried the Jesus child on his shoulders across a river. It was some time ago that he had learned this. But he wasn't so sure about Christian icons anymore.

He quickly went up the small slope to the castle, past the Ursula Nunnery and the Carmelita Church, and through the castle alley to Ludwigs Square, the big airy square that unfolds right after the narrow alley like a book being opened. To his left, Johann saw the massive pillars of the castle gate casting long shadows. Visitors only noticed this gate when they approached it from the east. In front of the gate, a banner fastened with two ropes proclaimed, "In Straubing, we greet with 'Heil Hitler.'" He saw the bold black letters on the light material and shivered, not sure if the cold he felt was from this sight or the icy wind. He turned to the right.

In the middle of the square was the town's tower, its five copper pinnacles and gigantic clock face with golden hands rising high above a row of patrician houses. Johann took off his leather gloves and blew into his hands. The stony mouths in the fish fountain spouted icicles instead of the rushing water of summertime. Only the sight of the old houses lit by orange, rusty red and yellow sunbeams made him feel a little warmer.

Everything could be so calm, so peaceful, he thought. Between the houses with their baroque windows, stepped gables, Madonna statues and inscriptions, red scraps of cloth fluttered—tiny swastika flags that homeowners and residents proudly hung out of their windows.

Johann entered one of the buildings and found Maier bent over a table, pulling the straps of a red rolled-up cloth slowly over the flagpole. He was so absorbed in the task that he didn't notice Johann coming into the dark room.

"What are you hanging up?" Johann asked, even though he already knew the answer.

Maier jumped, turned and laughed, "Oh, it's you. Just the flag of the party. I just want to get along with everyone and not have any trouble. You just have to adapt sometimes, right?"

Johann shook his head, his expression skeptical.

"You understand," Maier shrugged. "I have to feed my wife and children. If I don't do this, I won't be able to find work and …"

Before Maier could finish, Johann interrupted him. "Do you think your wife and children will be better off when you do this? Do you think we are better off when other people have to disappear? Do you think they are going on vacation? Maier, don't be so ignorant! They are being killed."

Maier looked pained but Johann couldn't stop himself. "You've got to know how this is going to go. The next ones that Hitler kills will be his own people." Johann could feel his heart race. Blood rushed to his face and his hands felt burning hot. He tried to breathe deeply.

Maier was not saying anything, as if he was waiting for Johann to come up with more words. For a couple of seconds, everything was silent.

Maier cleared his throat and scratched behind his ear. "Um, Johann, about the wooden bench. My wife and I are convinced that the old one will last. You don't have to make us a new one. You didn't have to come here. You also don't have to tell anyone that you were here."

Maier tried to grin a little and looked at Johann, who had only one burning thought. Maria told me to be careful. I promised her. And what do I end up doing? He bit his bottom lip and stared at the floor of the entrance hall.

"Of course, Maier, I will do that." Johann nodded his head. He looked once more over at the man bent again over the flag and then walked out of the room.

Outside, Johann couldn't help noticing the three long red flags with swastikas hanging from the upstairs windows, fluttering in the wind. The flags had been there for a few years. He had tried his best not to look at them, but now they were flapping right in front of his eyes, the red material, bright in the sun.

Several men with polished leather boots, black caps and long, dark coats stood in front of the local pub. Johann put his gloves on and tried to observe them without looking directly at them. Have they noticed me? he wondered. Are they talking about me? Again, he felt his heart beating faster. If he had his way, he would have gone over and yelled at them. But what good would that do? What would happen to him, Maria and the children?

Just as he was about to leave the square, he heard one of the men say, "We live in a significant time. This guy, he won't like it when the next war comes along. He doesn't even like our marches and songs." Another one laughed out loud and clapped the speaker on the shoulder in approval.

Johann stopped to glance at them again. Was it just his imagination or were they really looking at him? Leave quickly, just go, he thought and hurried across the square, back to the castle alley, past the Carmelita Church where people were just leaving the service, and back to the castle. There he turned around for the first time. Was he being followed? Did he imagine hearing footsteps behind him down the narrow alley? It's just your imagination—nobody is coming after you. He tried to calm his mind, standing alone by the fountain in the castle courtyard with only the wind whistling past.

The following night, Johann awoke again. As hard as he tried, he couldn't remember what he had just been dreaming. He wiped off the pearls of sweat from his forehead and sat up. Maria slept on, breathing deeply and evenly.

If only I could sleep like that, he thought. After a few minutes, he stood up, stepped into his fleece slippers, pulled on his dressing gown and walked to the window. Snowflakes whirled outside now; a strong wind had come up overnight. Icy around its edges, the windowpane hummed quietly whenever a burst of wind pushed against it. The whole street was covered in snow—almost twenty centimeters in one night. None of his neighbors' windows showed any light. Only the moon illuminated the empty streets.

Johann jumped when the bells of the Carmelita Church rang out—he had been concentrating on seeing if anyone was on the street.

Two o'clock in the morning, and I am standing at the window, he thought. He leaned forward, both forearms on the windowsill, to better see the entrance to his home. *Are those footsteps in the snow?* He pressed his face so close to the glass it steamed up. With the sleeves of his dressing gown, he wiped over the pane and squinted into the dark. There were marks in the snow, more than one. His eyes followed the trail—they had come from the town square.

Johann moved away from the window. What time had he gone to bed? It must have been 10 p.m., around the same time it started to snow. It couldn't have been very long ago that someone had stood in front of his door, since the marks were clearly visible from the window and not completely covered with snow yet.

His heartbeat sped up again, his hands shaking. He went back to the window and bent forward. The footsteps went from the street to the entrance. The fresh snow there was completely trampled.

He quietly walked across the dark bedroom floor on the balls of his feet and into the hall, closing the door behind him. He hurried down the stairs to the front door. Carefully, he put his ear to the wooden door. No, he couldn't hear anything.

Slowly, he pressed the door handle down and opened the door inwards, just wide enough to slip his head through the narrow opening. Along with the trampled new snow were two cigar stubs. He imagined he could still smell the earthy aroma of the cigars in the cold air.

The footsteps clearly led from the town square to his door and then away again. Whoever had been standing there in the middle of the night must have turned around to go back the same way. But who would visit him at this hour? Did any of his friends need help? But if they were friends, wouldn't they knock on his door? His sleep had been so restless lately that he was certain he would have heard someone knocking. And none of his friends smoked cigars.

Once again, he looked left and right—but the street was dark, and no one could be seen. He realized was shivering with cold in his thin dressing gown, so he closed the door and turned the key twice. He pressed his shoulder against the wooden door to make sure it was completely closed, then quietly slipped into the kitchen, where it was hardly warmer than outdoors.

Better not turn the light on, he thought, as he inched through the room by feeling his way along the stove. He had no desire to be in the bad books of the block warden, who would complain if a light came on anywhere. When he got past the stove, he stood on his toes, stretching to reach a metal box high on a shelf. He carefully lifted the green tin that had once held tea but was now dented and rusted. He opened the lid to see several typed flyers.

This hiding place is no longer safe, he thought. With the container under his arm, he went back into the hall. Halfway along the staircase, he knelt on the floor, lifted a floorboard and moved it to the side. In the hollow space below were a bundle of Reichsmarks and a pocket watch he had inherited from his father. He added the tin.

A couple of the flyers had already been distributed. Johann had handed one to a young man who dared to stand in front of a village shop and say that Hitler was going to start a war that would turn the entire world against Germany. Another flyer had gone to a father whose children played with Tilly and Hans and who was worried what would happen to them in the future.

Johann had slipped one of the flyers to Peter in the hope that he might change his mind. They had met on a Saturday afternoon on the Ludwigs Square and Peter had told him excitedly that the house beside his was now empty because a Jewish family had moved away. Peter reported that he had already talked to someone from the municipality and that he would be able to buy it for just a few Reichsmark. Peter had laughed and said that his children would live there one day, and what a stroke of good fortune it was.

Johann carefully moved the floorboard back into place and pressed down on the wood with the palm of his hand, securely wedging the board into place. He had to be sure even Maria wouldn't notice.

Sometime later in the night, he managed to go to sleep. When he woke up again, it was just getting light. He blinked and looked toward the window. The sky was thick with grey clouds. Through the haze, he could see smoke rising from his neighbor's chimney. The roof was covered in snow.

At this time of day, I would have been in my workshop already, sanding wood and sorting the bristles for making brushes, he thought. How he missed the smell of wood chips, missed being able to work in peace on his own. How much he had enjoyed walking through the shops, houses and pubs with a basket of brushes for sale.

Johann had always enjoyed gossiping with people and hearing the latest rumors from town. But these days, he found it difficult to talk or listen to them. When they told him that they finally had a decent job now, thanks to Hitler, he almost felt ill. Naturally, every one of them had an uncle who worked in Munich or Nürnberg in a factory or a nephew who managed to earn a few Reichsmark because they poured cement for the Reichsautobahn—the highway that was going to connect all corners of the country.

When Johann brought up the fact that they didn't have trade unions anymore, they shook their heads and called him crazy. When a haggard woman in the marketplace boasted that all four of her sons now had work because of Hitler, he asked if she believed her sons could be sure to leave the military service in one piece. She held the sugar beet she had just purchased up to his face and hissed at the saleswoman, "I am going to remember this man." Both women gave him stern looks and he simply turned around and left. But he worried. Did they know his name? He had seen the woman with the beets before; he just couldn't remember where.

When he came home that night, the children were already in bed. He turned on the radio in the living room to the local station, the Volksempfänger, one of the radio receivers developed by engineer Otto Griessing at the request of Propaganda Minister Joseph Goebbels. He turned down the sound and fooled around with the gadget until he could find some other frequencies, picking up snatches of music and other languages. He leaned over the radio and listened intently. The news wasn't good.

Later that morning, he had almost fallen back asleep when he heard Maria calling, "Johann, Johann, are you coming down? The coffee is ready." The kitchen smelled like freshly brewed coffee. Maria had already heated the stove with firewood. He wondered if she had noticed that the tea container was no longer on the shelf. Johann kissed her cheek and smiled. Maria pushed a steaming cup into his hand and sat on the wooden bench.

"There was some snowfall last night," she said.

He tried to act surprised and not think about the footprints. He went to the window and saw snowflakes still whirling around outside.

"Hmm, but you did go down to the door," Maria said. "Johann, don't you remember? I heard you when you got up."

Johann cleared his throat. "I'm sorry I woke you." He tried to smile. "I was thirsty and when I went downstairs, I checked to see how deep the snow in front of the door was." He took a sip of coffee and put the cup to the side. "Now I have to go outside and clear the snow."

"Hans and Tilly are already outside," she said, her tone brisk.

From the alcove beside the kitchen, Johann could hear Erwin babbling in his little bed. Maria went over to wrap him in a blanket and lift him up.

"I woke up long before you," Maria said as she carried Erwin back into the kitchen.

"He has trouble sleeping when it's so cold. He is always shaking off his blanket." Johann hoped his answer would be enough for her.

"That's not the reason I couldn't sleep," Maria said as she rocked the little one in her arms. "I heard men talking in front of the door."

"You must have been dreaming," Johann said quickly. He tried to stay calm, but his mind went spinning. Had his wife heard the voices of the men whose footprints he'd seen in the snow? And what was the reason they had stopped at his door in the middle of the night?

"They were probably drunk. Who else would be out walking in the streets in this weather?"

"No idea." Maria shrugged, but continued to look at him as if she wanted to study every movement of his face. "You would probably know that better than I," she added before turning away.

Later that morning, Johann took Tilly and Hans to the shores of the Danube. Tilly pulled a wooden sled her father had made for her. Hans played in the snow ahead of them, often turning around to throw snowballs at them.

On the river, the ice cracked as it was carried by the current, periodically bumping into rocks or other blocks of ice. Several ducks waddled along the shore and began chattering loudly when a couple of children threw rocks in their direction. They were the boys Johann had recently observed.

He brushed the snow off a wooden bench with the palm of his hand and sat down to watch Tilly and Hans dragging the sled across the open field. Across from them, in close proximity to the other children, a young couple walked past the castle. Johann could barely make out the Carmelita and St. Jacobs Church from his seat on the bench as the fog had moved in like a veil. Several black crows sat on a weeping willow with branches covered in frost that almost reached into the Danube. Johann narrowed his eyes to count the crows. There were five.

Tilly came running. Her cheeks were red with cold and there were tiny snowflakes in her hair.

"Father, who was killed here, again?" she asked in agitation and grabbed his sleeve.

"Agnes Bernauer. They drowned her in the Danube in the Middle Ages. We told you that over a hundred times already."

"Yes, that's right," Tilly said. But this didn't seem to be what she wanted to hear. "Was she Jewish?"

"Tilly, what kind of rubbish are you talking about?"

"The boy over there, he said that a Jew has been killed in Straubing." She pointed to a small slope where Hans was sledding. Another boy with a sled was standing nearby. Johann jumped up and stomped through the snow to the hill.

"Hey, you, what are you talking about?" he asked the boy, grabbing his shoulder.

"What do you mean?" The boy jerked away with a sharp movement.

"What are you saying about Jews?"

"My father said that they shot a Jew and that it had served him right," the boy said, grinning rudely.

"See to it that you get out of here," Johann said, his voice becoming louder. "This is not something I want to hear."

"I can say what I want. My father says all Jews deserve to be killed."

"Get lost this minute," Johann screamed at him.

This seemed too much for the boy, and he grabbed the rope of his sled and ran away. Tilly and Hans stared at their father with open mouths.

Johann tried to calm himself. "Did you recognize that boy?" he asked his children as he watched the boy run over the castle bridge in the direction of the town.

Both shook their heads.

"Why do Jews deserve to be killed, Father?" Tilly asked, her voice full of tears. "You are not supposed to kill anyone."

"Nobody says we should be killing anyone," said Johann, even though he realized this was no longer true. He pulled Tilly close and patted her head. She started sobbing. Hans sat on the sled and stared at his shoes.

Later that day, they all gathered at home in the kitchen. Tilly sewed a small cloth doll with Maria's help and Hans carried firewood into the house with his father. After their dinner of cabbage soup, Johann took the children to bed. They had avoided talking about the events of the morning once they were home, but Tilly again had tears in her eyes. "Father," she said, hugging her pillow and her little stuffed bear close. "Father, who was the boy talking about? Who was the Jew that was killed?"

"No one's been killed, Tilly, no one. Now go to sleep," Johann said and gave her a kiss on the forehead. She closed her eyes and wiped her tears with her hand.

Maria had already gone to bed. Johann sat in the armchair and turned the dial on the radio, which was crackling and hissing. As he tried to find a different frequency, he again thought of the boy by the river. Had he witnessed a Jew getting killed? Did someone tell him? Or was he only mindlessly repeating what he heard his father saying?

Four years earlier, when men dressed in black dragged Otto Selz from his home in Upper Bach Street and eventually shot him in a forest, Johann had realized what was happening. It had been mid-March 1933, only a few days after Hitler gained power in Bavaria. Selz was a Jewish cattle and goods dealer who had been harassed in articles in the Stürmer, a weekly Nazi newspaper published by Julius Streicher from 1923 to the end of World War II. Even today, almost four years later, nobody was sure who had invaded the Selz family home.

Yet from the moment Otto Selz disappeared, Johann knew that everyone who was different or who thought differently would soon have no place in this country. He knew that Hitler was not just screaming from the podium, but also encouraging murder, and that there were many willing to participate with actions as well as with words.

Was the boy talking about that murder?

It made Johann sad that some children mindlessly repeated what they heard others say, but at the same time, it made him proud that his children were different from them. He was glad to see that Tilly had seen this as wrong and that she asked about it.

The radio was still producing only a humming sound so Johann gave up trying to find a clear signal and turned it off, reluctantly going to bed.

He woke up in the dark to the sounds of muffled knocking and hammering.

"Johann, Johann, wake up," Maria whispered and shook him.

He was startled when he felt her cold hands on his shoulder.

"Johann. They are here," she wept.

For the first time in a long while, he had been sleeping deeply. It must still be very early in the morning, but now he could hear it clearly—a loud banging at the front door. Johann threw the blanket back, jumped up and ran to the window. He leaned forward and saw several men at the door.

"Open up. Schutzpolizei," one of them yelled, identifying the men as members of a branch of the Bavarian state police.

Johann turned around, went to the bed and grabbed Maria's shoulders

"Maria, listen to me," he said, his voice shaking. "You don't know anything. I never told you anything." In the dim moonlight he could make out the tears on Maria's cheeks, her face distorted by fear.

"Open up. Schutzpolizei!" someone yelled again. "Open up." The loud banging rattled the window.

Tilly threw the door to her parent's bedroom open. "Father, Father, somebody is at the door," she cried.

"Maria, you have to go to the children," Johann said loudly, giving his wife a quick, anxious hug.

Tilly stayed at the bedroom door as if rooted to the spot. Barefoot in a thin white cotton nightie, she held her little bear against her chest. Johann tore open the closet door, pulled on a warm knitted sweater and slipped into a pair of pants. Still barefoot, he ran downstairs.

When he reached the bottom stair, the front door burst open with a loud crash. Icy air and snow blew into the room. Five men dressed in long black coats crowded in the doorway.

The first one took a big step inside. He seemed to be in charge. "You two look upstairs," he ordered, pointing at the two men standing on the left. "You two take downstairs," he told the others.

Obediently, two men pushed past Johann to run upstairs, their heavy boots thundering.

Tilly, Hans and Maria, with Erwin in her arms, stood at the top of the stairs. Nobody was screaming or sobbing anymore, just silent tears running down their cheeks. They held each other tight. Then little Erwin started whimpering.

The two men stormed past them, one into the bedroom, the other into the children's room. Johann could hear them tearing open closet doors, throwing things on the ground, stomping around with their heavy boots.

Something heavy hit the bedroom floor and Johann guessed it was the mattress.

Downstairs, he could hear the other two smashing dishes and moving the wooden bench.

The leader confronted Johann, his long coat open and billowing with each step. "Where are you hiding the flyers?" he shouted.

The only thing Johann could see of his face was his narrow, chapped lips. His eyes were hidden in the shadow of the dark cap.

"I do not know what you are talking about," Johann answered calmly. One thing reassured him amidst all the chaos and noise: the floorboard blended in perfectly with the rest of the floor.

"We know you have been handing out flyers that say rubbish about our Führer," the leader bellowed. "You are now under arrest."

He grabbed Johann's arm and tried to pull him out of the hallway. With one hand, Johann held the bannister so that he could get one last glimpse of his family. They huddled close together at the top of the stairs, crying. Erwin screamed and flailed. Tilly reached out and whispered, "Father, no."

Johann turned around and addressed the leader. "Why are you doing this? I haven't done anything to you."

The man laughed and yanked harder. The two from upstairs clomped down the stairs and the other two hurried into the hallway from the kitchen. Together, they pushed him out through the open door, so that he ended up barefoot in the snow.

"Don't do this," Johann said. "Please, just leave me here with my family."

They pushed him into a black van parked directly in front of the house and sped away.

Johann lay in a heap on the floor of the van wondering where they were taking him. The car stopped after a short trip over what felt like cobblestone streets.

"Out with you," said the leader. "Everyone needs to see what happens to someone like you." He opened the door and pulled him out.

Johann could hardly believe his eyes. The car stood right in front of the Holy Trinity Column in the Theresien town square. A few market stalls were already set up and many people from Straubing were on their way to work. The sky was grey, and in the gloom, not even the golden top of the Holy Trinity Column shone.

Johann stood barefoot in the frozen square and pulled his toes in.

Two of the men grabbed him by the arms and pushed him forward. The other two leaned casually against the van and smoked cigars.

"We don't want people like you here," screamed the leader and ripped Johann's knitted sweater open. "A dirty friend of the Jews."

The others laughed. One of them drove his knee into Johann's back, and he crumpled. He was kneeling on the icy ground, trying to get up, when his gaze fell on a couple that was strolling by. The young woman looked away as if ashamed, but the man stared at Johann with curiosity and a grin. An old woman stopped and stared at him with an open mouth. Two boys wearing paperboy hats whispered and giggled, pointing their fingers at him.

"These kinds of traitors are not wanted in our society," the leader proclaimed. "Heil Hitler." He stood at attention and lifted his right hand in the Hitler greeting.

He brought down his hand to push Johann so hard that he fell to the ground again. The leader's eyes glittered, he seemed to relish the excitement.

Johann looked around. Was there no one who would come to his aid? Not one? A couple of strong, young men stood nearby. It would be simple for them to challenge the group, but they continued smoking their cigarettes, heads bowed, and looked sheepishly at the cobblestones.

Still on the icy pavement, Johann noticed a small figure out of the corner of his eye. Who was that peeking out from behind the Holy Trinity Column? He narrowed his eyes and recognized Sarah, the six-year-old child of a Jewish family Johann knew well. He had slipped her mother a few pieces of coal and some carrots a couple of days ago. The Nazis had taken the father away two years ago. Since then, the family fought to survive daily

Sara regarded him with big brown eyes, her little knitted cap pulled tight over her black hair. Her woolen mittens were full of holes and the soles of her small leather shoes hung loose.

Every time the leader shouted, she disappeared behind one of the pillars. When it was quiet for a moment, she leaned forward and looked at Johann.

After a while, the crowd grew as more citizens of Straubing came to see what the bellowing, pushing and shoving was all about. Some looked scared. Some recognized Johann from when they had bought his woodwork or talked to him in the market square. Some walked past him with apathetic, empty expressions. But one after the other, some with hesitation, others with enthusiasm, lifted their right arm and joined in with the leader's "Heil Hitler!"

Elke

In February 1937 the National Socialists brought my grandfather, Johann, to the concentration camp in Dachau. Heinrich Himmler had built it four years before to imprison people who dared speak up against Hitler. For two years, my grandfather was interned, humiliated and abused by his Nazi captors. Trapped in a camp surrounded by a high-voltage electric fence and watchtowers, he was at the mercy of Nazi brutality, like thousands of others. He suffered from the cold and hunger. He watched people die.

But he survived.

Two years later, in 1939, he was released from what the Nazis called "protective custody." But his humiliation did not end there. In 1941 Johann was forced to join the German army's Afrika Korps under the leadership of Erwin Rommel, known in Nazi propaganda as the Desert Fox.

Johann was forced to put his life on the line for causes he didn't support, for an ideology that had torn him from his family. At the battle of El Alamein in 1942, he was seriously wounded. After many months in a military hospital in Africa, he finally made it back to Straubing at the end of the war—with three bullet wounds: his stomach, his shoulder and one of his lungs. These wounds would never heal fully, and he continued to suffer from stomach bleeds and breathing problems. Sixteen years later, he took his last breath, a man in his early fifties.

This is my grandfather Johann, who objected to Hitler's propaganda and as a result was sent to the concentration camp in Dachau from 1937 to 1939.

Chapter 3

An existence as brittle as frost-covered sticks

Tilly, Gstütt, 1938

THE MOMENT THE NAZIS DRAGGED HER FATHER OUT OF the house, Tilly knew he could no longer protect her. Not from mean little boys like those at the sled hill, not from men in black clothing. As her father was shoved into a black van, she understood that her childhood was over. At the age of nine, she knew it was her responsibility to help her mother. She would have to look after her younger siblings.

Standing at the top of the stairs, clinging to Maria, Tilly felt her mother shaking. She never saw her mother smile again.

Every night, Tilly folded her hands under the bedcovers. Erwin and Hans already asleep, she prayed, "Dear God, I am not sure what they have done with Father. I really don't know. I will do everything you want me to do. You might have noticed how well I am looking after Erwin and Hans. Please bring our father back. We miss him so. And we need him."

In the evenings, Tilly imagined what it would be like when her father came home. Her mother would not have to work so hard, doing laundry and sewing for other people. She could be home more often and wouldn't be so sad. Maybe they could even finish sewing the doll that lay on the table next to her bed since that terrible night, when one of the men in black trampled it. How she longed to sit in the warm room next to her mother, to lean against her and listen as she read stories from the old book of fairy tales. Her father would sit in the armchair and she would join him after a while. She would sit on his knee to play Hoppe Reiter, one of her favorite games, where you bounced on someone's knee as if you're riding a horse until you're unseated. To end the game, her father would let her fall, catching her just before she reached the ground.

Every night, she fell asleep with these memories, but when she woke up the next morning, they seemed far away—almost as if they had never existed.

Tilly opened her eyes. The tip of her nose felt frozen. The air in the room was so cold that breathing hurt a little and her mouth felt dry. When she swallowed, her tonsils stung. She watched her breath turning into a small cloud, slowly rising in the air above her bed. It was snowing outside, just like the night they had come for her father more than a year ago.

Besides the absence of her father, there was another difference. Now the window in the children's room was frozen, inside and outside. In the moonlight, the glass looked milky. Ice crystals covered the window, making it look beautiful. Almost like the expensive lace veil of a bride, thought Tilly.

But the beauty came with terrible cold. She kicked off her warm covers and jumped out of bed. She wore her thick hand-knitted wool socks all night now. They were itchy, but at least they warmed her feet as much as possible. Her growing feet had stretched the material so thin that her big toes pushed through holes that also grew bigger every day. In the dark, Tilly felt her way through the room, eased the door open and pushed her way through a small gap so she could close the door quickly behind her.

"Whatever you do, don't let more cold into the room," her mother had told her, because it was even colder in the hallway.

Every time she went from the children's room to the stairs, she remembered standing on the landing with her mother, Hans and Erwin. She never forgot her last glimpse of her father; how he had clutched the bannister so he could look at them one last time. Tilly had waved at him, before the man with the long coat and the black cap had torn him away.

In the dark kitchen, her mother knelt in front of the stove with a candle.

"Come in and close the door quickly," she whispered.

Tilly quietly closed the kitchen door.

Maria lit a crumpled piece of newspaper with the candle and threw it into the stove. "Tilly, we have to find some firewood today. It just keeps getting colder and colder."

"I can look in the Vogelau forest. I am sure I will find a few branches there," Tilly replied. No matter how cold it was in the Vogelau and how much she hated stomping through the deep snow to tug at branches and twigs to loosen them and drag them home, she would do it. She tried to smile so her mother wouldn't be able to tell how hard this task was for her.

"But don't let them catch you. They don't like to see that," Maria cautioned, giving her daughter a stern look.

The newspaper crackled and burst into a bright orange flame before curling up and turning black. In the stove, the firewood crackled. Tilly didn't want to look away. Just staring at it made her feel warmer. She held her hands, covered in thin woolen mittens, close to the opening in the stove. The warmth made her feel good, and she stretched her toes, which had been curled inwards since she got up. The ends of her fingers and toes felt as if someone was poking them with hundreds of tiny pins. But she could not relax fully—she remembered that even feeling that little bit of warmth wasn't safe.

Just recently, there had been a loud banging on the front door late one bitterly cold evening. Tilly had bundled herself up in her blanket and crept to the landing to see what was happening.

Her mother had opened the door and a gruff-looking man barked at her. "How are you doing without your husband? Everyone knows about him, and how his opinions have landed him in jail." His crooked mouth looked as if he would burst out laughing any minute. "And you should know better than to waste firewood. You never know how long this will have to last for you!"

Maria banged the door shut in his face.

"This will have consequences," the man threatened from behind the door.

"See that you get away from here," Maria called back.

"What a mess this is," he hollered in response, banging once more on the door for good measure. Then she heard him stomp off through the snow.

Leaning against the inside of the door, Maria slid to the floor and started to cry.

Tilly, still wrapped in her bedcovers against the cold, went downstairs to hug her mother.

"Mama, don't cry," she whispered. She stroked Maria's face with her cold fingers. "Father will come back. I can feel it." Tilly sat down on the cold stone floor beside her mother and folded her into the blanket for warmth, hugging her mother as tightly as she could.

Tilly played that moment over and over again in her mind. How much she had wanted to comfort her mother, to hold her close. But Maria just sat on the wooden bench with a fleece blanket over her shoulders. Leaning as close as possible to the dim light of a candle, she tried to pull the thread through the eye of her sewing needle. With fingers stiff and shaking from the cold, Maria had to try over and over again, breathing into her hands to warm them. On the table in front of her was a pile of white cotton clothing, the night clothes, slips and undergarments of a woman whose husband held a high rank in the SS.

Maria had soaked the laundry in bleach for three days. She had placed the tub close to the stove, but even so, it was lucky that the water didn't freeze. She couldn't even imagine what would happen if the lingerie had been ruined. After that, the undergarments had hung on a clothesline in the kitchen, the only reasonably warm place in the house. This morning, after two days, they were finally dry.

Now, Maria mended the holes and sewed on a few buttons that had come off, carefully stitching up the fine fabric.

Tilly sat next to her on the wooden bench. She wondered who could wear something this flimsy in the winter. They must have a really warm home, she thought. Tilly's stomach was growling. She cut herself a narrow slice of bread from the dark loaf that had already gone a little hard.

"Leave some for Hans," her mother said.

Tilly nodded. She had been hungry all night but didn't want her mother to know. Maria opened a jar of rosehip jam, releasing a sweet, fruity aroma. She scraped a small amount of jam out with a knife, leaving only a little bit at the bottom of the jar.

Tilly remembered the sunny fall day she had collected the rose hips with her father. It had been so nice to walk among the colorful trees, past the Vogelau, and look for ripe rosehips in the bushes. That afternoon, they all worked together in the kitchen, cooking jam and canning it in glass jars. The wine-red jam tasted sweet and sour at the same time and stuck to their lips and the corners of their mouths. But now the last jar was nearly empty.

"When I come home from school, I will go straight to the Vogelau and look for wood," Tilly said before taking a bite of her bread.

"Good, I will finish the wash and go into town later. Someone wants me to make them a tablecloth and curtains. Can you watch Erwin then?"

Tilly nodded. She focused on her last bite of bread with jam. She tried to make it last and promised herself she'd never forget the taste on her tongue.

Tilly used to love going to school. She had loved packing her satchel in the morning, getting a kiss from her mother and running across the castle bridge as quickly as possible. There Frieda would be waiting, her friend from town, with long blond braids and freckled face. Together, they strolled to school along the Danube, startling the ducks. In the classroom, they sat on the bench side by side, and when the teacher wasn't looking, they exchanged whispers and giggles. When Frieda forgot her slate once, Tilly pushed hers toward her friend. Frieda brought her a candy the next day to return the favor.

But now Frieda was no longer talking to her.

Two days after her father was picked up by the men in black clothes, Tilly waited for Frieda on the bridge. So close to the duke's castle, it was icy cold, with a sharp wind whistling in her face. Was Frieda sick or had something happened to her? Tilly kept looking at the slope, hoping her friend would come running around the corner soon. But Frieda simply didn't show up.

After waiting for what seemed a long time, Tilly rushed along the riverbank toward her school. Despite the cold air, her brown curls stuck to her forehead and sweat trickled down her back. The wind whipped her face, turning her cheeks a bright red. Every breath stabbed her lungs, but she needed to keep running to get to school on time. She ran the whole way. The schoolbag on her back bounced, and twice she tripped over a pile of snow. Getting up from a fall, she noticed her woolen mittens were wet and her knee was scraped. Even worse, she had a hole in the thick black stocking over her right knee.

Oh, no, what will Mother say? Tilly thought. What do I look like?

She was panting as she ran into the schoolhouse. Her first thought was to go to the teacher and alert him that something had happened to Frieda. Frieda had never missed school, and she had almost never walked there alone. Frieda was someone you could depend on. Something must have happened to her.

Tilly opened the heavy wooden door to her classroom with the last of her strength. She stood in the doorway, hole in her stockings, sweaty, red faced and without a hat, which she had lost somewhere along the way. Everybody turned to stare at her.

The lesson had already begun, and the teacher stood at the blackboard with a piece of chalk in his hand. He sniffed and wanted to know why Tilly was late. Just as Tilly was starting to tell him about her concerns that something had happened to Frieda, she saw her friend sitting in the classroom. But today Frieda was sitting in a different row, not in her usual seat beside Tilly. And like the other kids, she stared at Tilly with an indifferent expression.

After that day, Tilly had sat on her bench alone. The space beside her remained empty. Frieda never spoke to her again. Tilly now took a different route to get to school and no longer enjoyed attending.

She also realized that it was much harder for Hans. She heard that a boy from his class had spit on Hans and screamed, "Your father is in jail." The other boys had laughed. This was another thing they never talked to their mother about.

At the end of the school day her classmates stood in front of the building with the big windows. They gossiped, laughed and whispered secrets to each other. Tilly was never included. One day a year later, she almost cried, it had hurt so much. But she had grown used to it to the point where it almost didn't matter anymore. Tilly knew that they didn't speak to her because her father had been taken to Dachau. At the same time, she had no idea why this would be a reason for shunning her. But what could she say to them?

Tilly also noticed that the teacher didn't call on her in class. And she wasn't doing as well as before, even though she studied hard. Sometimes, Tilly was jealous of Frieda and the others, whose fathers marched across the town square in their uniforms.

Frieda's father even drove up at the end of the school day in an elegant black car and stopped in front of the school. He emerged from the driver's side, closed the buttons on his black leather jacket and straightened the black cap where the Death Head skull glittered. Frieda ran across the street to him. "Father, Father," she shouted, delight in her voice. He bent down to give her a kiss on the cheek, stroked her shining hair and took her satchel.

On the first floor of the school, a window opened. The teacher looked out and waved eagerly until Frieda's father saw him. "Heil Hitler," the teacher shrieked from above and raised his right arm.

"Heil Hitler," Frieda's father answered, raising his right arm and bringing his heels together so that his black boots clicked.

Snuggled against her father, Frieda smiled.

Tilly stared at them from the other side of the road. How she would have liked to be in their place. It would be so nice to have her father around and be picked up in such a fancy car. Surely, Frieda's mother didn't have to work as hard as her own, and at Frieda's house, they most likely had something warm to eat—maybe even a roast.

"What a dashing man," Tilly heard a woman whisper behind her.

Turning around, she recognized her classmate Anne's mother. The woman's cheeks were turning rosy and she smiled at Frieda's father across the street. She straightened her woolen jacket and smoothed her shoulder-length blond hair.

"Anne," the woman said, "don't you want to invite Frieda over some time?"

Anne beamed and said, "Oh, yes, may I?"

"Of course, let's ask them," her mother said, pushing Anne ahead of her across the street.

Tilly watched how Anne's mother shook hands with Frieda's father and even bent her legs into a small curtsy. As she pushed Anne closer to Frieda, she addressed Frieda's father, shrugging her shoulders and shaking her hair like a young girl, sometimes laughing out loud. Frieda's father continued standing at attention, and his face showed clearly how flattered he was.

Tilly turned and walked away. This afternoon, Anne and Frieda would play together at Frieda's house, where it was probably cozy and warm, and nobody had to huddle in bed with a fleece blanket over their shoulders. Why couldn't her father be like that? What in the world had he done that he was no longer allowed to stay at home?

Tilly was furious. She quickly walked across the castle bridge, looking down at the snow-covered ground. She didn't want to see anything else today—no ducks, no Danube, no other children. After crossing the castle bridge, she turned right, into the Vogelau. She came across a pool of water that had been frozen for many weeks. During the summer, you could hear frogs and mosquitos, but now it was quiet. The echo of Anne's mother's fake laughter rang in her ears.

Nobody had been walking in the Vogelau for a while. With the snow reaching to her knees, every step was difficult for Tilly. Her shoes and even her stockings felt wet. They had never dried completely after water had seeped through the hole in her shoe in the morning.

Behind an old tree stump covered with frost, Tilly discovered a few bushes where the branches were easy to reach and usable for firewood. She stomped closer, the snow crunching under her feet. Suddenly, she heard rustling. Was it an animal? Tilly stopped, peeking out from behind the tree trunk. What she saw startled her. Next to the bushes stood a girl with black hair and a dark jacket. The girl, who was smaller than Tilly, had to stand on her toes to reach high enough to be able to pull down the branches, which were shedding snow. Tilly could see that she wore woolen mittens with holes and had a big hole in her stockings. Beside the little girl lay a small pile of branches that she had likely gathered.

As if she felt Tilly looking at her, the girl looked around and took a step back. She froze, watching Tilly intently with big brown eyes.

"You don't have to be scared," Tilly said quietly, stepping out from behind the tree trunk. "I'm only here to gather a few branches, just like you."

The girl still stared at her, but she finally nodded.

"Look, I'll help you," said Tilly. She stepped closer to the shrub, reached for some higher branches and broke them off. She took a bundle and pressed it into the girl's arms.

Up close, Tilly could see the yellow star with the six points that was sewn on the girl's jacket. She knew this meant that the girl was a Jew.

The girl took a step back, but kept her eyes glued to Tilly's face.

Tilly looked around. What would people say if they saw her helping a Jew? Would she get into trouble? But there was no one else there. And her father had always told her that all people were equal. He even had friends who were Jews.

Tilly smiled at the girl. "Let's keep going—there are more bushes up there."

Together they tromped through the snow. The girl's shoes and jacket were even more threadbare and torn than Tilly's. Her lips were blue, her face white as chalk. How long had she been in the Vogelau?

In a big field, they found some bushes with thin protruding branches. Tilly tore them off and threw the branches behind her, while the girl gathered everything into a big pile. They worked together until Tilly couldn't feel her fingers and her jacket was covered in snow, which was now falling heavily.

"Take as much as you need," Tilly told the girl, pointing at the pile.

The girl bent down, stuffed a couple of smaller twigs into her jacket pockets and picked up a bundle with both hands.

Tilly gathered the rest. Together they made their way back, trying to walk in their old footsteps so that they didn't sink deeper into the snow. The wind was so icy Tilly could hardly keep her eyes open and the snowflakes swirled around her face. She waited by the frozen pond to give the girl a chance to catch up.

Then Tilly asked, "What's your name?"

The girl, who had not spoken a single word while they were gathering branches, whispered, "Sara." She smiled and suddenly began running in the direction of the castle bridge.

"Wait," Tilly called after her. "Why are you running away?"

When Sara passed a fork in the road leading to the bridge, she lost a small branch.

Tilly arrived a few moments later and bent down to pick it up. A rosehip hung from the branch, covered with ice crystals but still a vibrant red. Tilly pinched the rosehip off with her fingernails. Carefully, she laid it in her left hand and patted it with her fingers. How beautiful it was. How brightly the red shone, even though it was covered by frost. Tilly lifted the rosehip between two fingers and gently placed it in her jacket pocket.

Her mother was already waiting for her at home, wearing her overcoat and her best leather shoes. Even though her things were old and had been repaired a few times, her mother still looked beautiful and charming, Tilly thought, as she walked through the door with the branches.

"Thank you, Tilly. We will have to dry them first," Maria said as she took a bundle. "I have to go into town. Erwin is sleeping in his bed. Please watch him. And Hans will probably want a piece of bread later on."

Her mother gave her a hasty kiss on the forehead and disappeared through the front door with a basket. Before Tilly spread the branches out on the kitchen table and gave Erwin a warmer blanket in his crib, she pulled the rosehip out of her pocket and placed it on her nightstand beside her doll. It was now her most prized possession.

Chapter 4

Poster of a German Mother

Maria, Hans, Tilly and Erwin
Straubing, 1939–1945

ON THE WAY TO THE CITY, MARIA DID HER BEST TO KEEP her balance to avoid falling with the basket. It held the freshly washed and repaired garments of the wife of the SS man. A little farther along, on a brick wall, was a poster of a blonde woman laughing, a healthy blond child in her arms. Something about "the German mother" was written in big Gothic letters underneath. Maria didn't want to read any of it. She concentrated on the icy ground and kept trudging along.

That would suit the men in uniform, she thought. Women were supposed to produce many sons so the Nazis could recruit them into the party. As if that's all the German mother was good for. Who was biking to the fields early in the morning in all kinds of wind and weather to convince the farmers to sell them another carrot or a cabbage? Who was begging to fix clothes or sew curtains for some spoiled wealthy lady? Who had not had a proper meal in months, so that her children wouldn't go hungry?

Almost every evening she put herself in danger as people stood in her doorway, wanting readings from her.

"Maria, you always know the right thing to do. Should I marry the young man from my neighborhood? Does he love me?"

"Maria, I really need your advice. What is wrong with me?"

People came to her with all kinds of things—even though her husband was "a jailbird," as they hissed behind her back. Even though only gypsies were fortune tellers and it was actually forbidden, what else could she do? Even a local policeman gave her a few Reichsmarks for her advice. Should she turn that away?

Already her mother, Lucia, had raised her and her four siblings through the first World War that way. Lucia's husband, Maria's father, had died in this war and—just like Maria now—had to depend on herself. So, she had set up a small hidden room in the attic while the war still raged. With every step, the old timber floorboard creaked. Dark heavy curtains were hung over the skylight and a dripping candle was placed on the table. On a wooden shelf stood a few books decorated with ornaments and pictures. Grownups had to walk bent over in the attic to avoid hitting their head on a wooden beam.

Maria always discovered the most wondrous things in the cards—sometimes showing a sun, or a king or even a devil.

Even though she was frightened of the devil, the attic with its squeaking trap door was Maria's favorite hiding place as a child. At first, she had never quite understood what her mother was doing up there. Almost every day, people came to them. First, they crept furtively through the yard and then climbed the small hidden staircase to the attic. Men with war wounds, pregnant women, old farm ladies, and even a priest. Once Maria helped an old lady down the wooden staircase, who stroked Maria on the cheek and said, "Your mother helped me a lot. I know what I should do now." Even as a child, Maria had not understood why it was forbidden to help people. That is why she always listened to everyone who came to her door and asked for advice.

When Maria thought of her mother, she smiled. It was the only thing that cheered her up on this day. The snow flurries had gotten worse and she had to be careful that she didn't slip and fall. She arrived at her customer's house and rang the doorbell.

The wife of the SS man opened it. "How nice that you are here. Please come in." The lady wore a thin beige satin dress; a long pearl necklace dangled around her neck. Her dark hair had been permed. She smiled at Maria. "Would you like a coffee? I just brewed some."

"No, thank you, Frau Schmidt. I just wanted to bring you your laundry," Maria said.

"I won't take no for an answer. Please come in, you look completely frozen through." The lady smiled and waved Maria in.

In the hallway, it was warm, almost stifling. The lady walked ahead and with every one of her movements, the material in her satin dress seemed to flow in a different direction. Her stiletto heels clicked on the tile floor. What an elegant lady, thought Maria to herself.

The lady turned around. "Please, may I have your coat?"

Maria was worried. Under her coat, she wore an old cotton dress that she had had to mend again just a week ago.

"No, I will leave my coat on, thank you," she said self-consciously.

"Please, give it to me," said the lady and reached out with both hands.

Maria unbuttoned her coat hesitantly and handed it to the lady, who hung it in her closet directly beside her brown mink coat. They went into the living room where a fire crackled in the fireplace. A porcelain coffee set decorated with small roses was already on the glass table. From the ceiling hung a chandelier with countless dangling glass crystals, a fur throw was placed on the couch, and in a display case stood rows of books with colorful covers and gold lettering.

"Please have a seat," said Frau Schmidt, pouring Maria a cup of steaming coffee. The woman's black hair gleamed under the light of the chandelier.

How long had it been since she was able to sit in a warm room like this, thought Maria as she took a sip. When she placed the cup back on the saucer, she had a closer look at the book lying right beside it. *Mein Kampf* by Adolf Hitler. Of course, she thought to herself, and tried to control her expression.

"I will take that away," said Frau Schmidt, picking it up and placing it on the display case. "My husband always reads from it."

Maria tried to smile politely and tugged at her cotton skirt uncomfortably.

"I wanted to ask you something." The lady's voice became softer. "I have heard that you are a good judge of things, and that you can truly help someone. That you can interpret some things …" She leaned over the glass table and looked meaningfully at Maria.

How should she react to that? Maria thought. In front of her sat the wife of an SS man who could betray her at any moment. But she could also take it badly if Maria didn't give her any advice.

At the same time, Frau Schmidt was always generous to her, and had always given her a few extra Reichsmarks. Before she finished pondering, the woman continued, whispering, "I am concerned about my husband." She turned around and looked in the direction of the window, as if she wanted to check to see if anyone was standing there. "Whenever he comes back from Dachau, he has nightmares. He screams in his sleep. Something is bothering him."

Dachau—the name hit Maria like a punch in the gut. Every night she tried to suppress thoughts of that camp and what they could be doing to Johann there. A lot of rumors floated around. Maria had been told how they had abused Johann by the Holy Trinity Column in the town square, that he was kicked and beaten. What would they do to him when no one was watching?

"What do you mean?" Maria asked, trying not to let her emotions show. Her stomach dropped and her pulse pounded.

"Something terrible must be happening there." The woman shrugged her shoulders and looked at Maria questioningly.

"Do you know what your husband does there?" asked Maria as quietly and calmly as she could.

"His command falls under the duties of the SS. Himmler arranged it like that. I think he looks at documents and sometimes does inspection rounds."

Did the woman know that Johann was imprisoned there? Maybe the SS man had seen him? He could probably let her know how he was doing.

"Maybe," Maria whispered very slowly, "maybe he is seeing things that make him feel scared." She paused for a second, the woman staring at her spellbound. "I don't want to offend you, but maybe he sees things that he doesn't approve of."

"What do you mean by that?" The woman's eyes widened. She set the cup that she was just about to drink from back on the table with a loud clack.

"Maybe your husband has to do things that bother his conscience?" As soon as Maria said it, she bit her lip. Now she had blabbed too much; she would have to be more careful. Every single word, every sentence could betray her.

"What could he possibly be doing that bothers his conscience?" she said loudly. "What do you mean? It is just a jail." The lady waved her arm dismissively, so that her bracelets chimed, and her pearl necklace flung sideways.

"One hears things …" said Maria. Suddenly it was quiet with only the crackling of the fire. "Some prisoners have died there." Maria swallowed.

"Died of what?" Frau Schmidt's voice began to shake.

"In Dachau. In custody," Maria answered quietly.

"But they were likely ill. Or they did something to harm themselves, because, because …"

What could Maria possibly say? If she let her know what a neighbor had secretly whispered to her over the garden fence recently, the woman could lose her composure and get Maria locked up as well. She had to keep her children in mind; she had to remain calm.

"Yes, of course. That is possible," Maria said, twisting her face into a polite smile. She stood up. "I have to get going. I am glad that you liked the things. I will get my coat." Maria left the living room and went to the wardrobe. Grabbing her coat, she forced herself to turn around once more and nod politely as she opened the door.

Frau Schmidt ran to the door. Her skin seemed ashen. She grabbed Maria's shoulder and held tight. "He is a good man," she said beseechingly, as if she wanted to convince Maria.

"I am sure he cares a great deal about you," Maria managed to answer quietly as her sweaty hands twisted the handle of her empty basket. The woman stood in the doorway, one hand on the door frame. She watched as Maria hurried through the front garden and across the snow-covered street. "A good man ..." she whispered after her.

Maria did not dare to visit the woman after that afternoon. She wouldn't even risk going near. She could not trust herself that next time she wouldn't scream at the woman, "Wake up and see what's really happening around you!" When she had to deliver an embroidered tablecloth nearby, she took a secret path, past an old barn and through an abandoned garden, to avoid walking by the house.

One Saturday morning, as Maria carried a paper bag of beef bones home to make soup, she saw the woman and her SS husband on the other side of the square. The sun was shining, and many people were out. For the first time in months, they were able to go into the city without mittens and thick knitted scarves to drink half a beer and chat a bit. Some bought their sweethearts the colorful cut flowers the market women were offering once again. Maria immediately noticed the lady, her expression making her stand out from the crowd.

Two little boys ran past the couple, laughing and shrieking and passing a ball back and forth. Another young pair had stopped walking, their eyes closed, savoring the sun that warmed their faces.

The SS man and his wife walked by the young pair. Frau Schmidt walked head down and tight lipped. She wore a perfectly tailored black suit; a brown box-shaped leather handbag dangled from her forearm and her black hair peeped out from under her dark satin hat. Her left arm was hooked tightly under her husband's, as if she wanted to hold him back. He strode on while she tried to keep pace in her high heels. His black leather coat was open on this spring day, and the silver buttons of his uniform sparkled in the sun. He looked straight ahead, and his lips were also pressed in a tight line.

Maria watched them out of the corner of her eye. Suddenly the woman lifted her head and looked straight at her. Maria would have liked to disappear behind the paper bag, but there was no way to hide. The woman did not turn her gaze away. She seemed to be walking slower. Her husband rushed forward, paying no attention to her. When he had dragged her directly opposite Maria, the lady leaned back a bit, peeked out from behind his coat and smiled at Maria. From her glance Maria knew that she didn't have to be scared; the woman would not betray her.

Less than nine months later, Hitler attacked Poland and plunged the whole world into war. Maria heard a voice rumble out of the wireless on that early morning in September—from now on, said the voice, they would be shooting back. Maria sat on Johann's old easy chair with her cup of coffee, the wireless crackling and popping, the voice of the Führer screeching. Her husband had been right. She gently stroked the cover of the easy chair with her hand. Johann had predicted that all the commotion and marching, all the torture and harassment, would eventually lead to war. It wouldn't be enough to shout and threaten, he'd said.

From the window, she could hear voices, some speaking loudly, some whispering quietly. On the street, neighbors were sharing recent news. Many were just as shocked as Maria, but nobody dared to say anything. What was going to happen to Johann in Dachau? What should she be doing with Tilly, Hans and Erwin? These were thoughts that haunted Maria for the next few months. When she heard the loud voice on the wireless proclaiming that the German Wehrmacht had rolled over Poland, Maria was in no mood to rejoice.

Maria bent over the washtub, scrubbing a white cotton blanket on the ridged board. A neighbor had just told her that the Wehrmacht had conquered Norway. They were acting as if they have conquered the entire world, thought Maria. She shook her head and continued scrubbing. She was able to hang her laundry outside again; she just had to try and catch a few sunny hours. In the grass next to the tub, yellow dandelions and white daffodils bloomed and long, light green shoots dangled from the hazelnut shrubs. She shook out the blanket and hung it over a rope she'd stretched out in the garden, pinching it in place with wooden clothespins. With both hands, she grabbed the blanket by the corners and pulled firmly so that it would dry with as few wrinkles as possible.

She heard a sound behind her, footsteps in the wet grass. Someone had plodded into the garden. Is Hans home from school already? Maria thought to herself, turning around.

In front of her stood Johann.

At first, she just gaped, then the wooden pin in her hand fell to the grass. Her feet felt like lead; she couldn't move them.

"Maria," he whispered and took a step toward her. Maria still could not move. She just stared at him—in a dirty coat, faded at the elbows, with a torn seam and two missing buttons. His filthy pants had vertical blue and white stripes and his shoes were worn out, the big toe of his left foot sticking out.

"Maria," he said a little louder. He had a deep scar on his left cheek and his throat was covered in long scratches. His lips were cracked and lined, and his skin was a sickly grey, just like the hair on his temples. In only two years, her young, strong Johann had become frail and looked much older. Then they fell into each other's arms.

When Hans and Tilly came back from school that afternoon, they could hardly believe who was sitting in the kitchen with Erwin on his lap. They stood in the doorway, sobbing and laughing, then ran to hug their father tightly. They held onto each other as they watched his every movement and word. They stroked his face and grabbed his hands just to be sure that he really was back with them again. They tried to smell him, to feel his warmth, soak up his voice—everything they had missed so much in the last couple of years.

When Tilly and Hans went to their room that night, they lay in their beds exhausted. Their bodies felt heavy, as if they had cried too much, so great was their happiness on one side and their fear on the other.

Their father looked thin and tortured. He seemed depressed, scared and intimidated. No matter how many times they asked him that day what it was like in Dachau, what they did with him there, if he suffered, if he wanted to go to a doctor the next day, he hadn't answered. He just repeated quietly, "They have released me from custody." He said he wanted to hear how Tilly and Hans were doing at school, if they had been studying hard, if Erwin was healthy and if they had enough to eat.

The last thing Tilly saw before her eyes closed that night was the rosehip on her nightstand, now dry and shriveled. It was no longer a bright red, but it was still there. Tilly smiled and fell asleep.

Johann never spoke to them about what happened to him in Dachau.

It didn't take long. The National Socialists occupied Paris, and then they drafted Johann into the Wehrmacht. In October 1940 he had to say goodbye to his family a second time. This time he wasn't dragged out and beaten, but for him, Maria, Tilly and Hans, it felt the same. Again, they stood in the hallway clutching each other, tears running down their cheeks. It was reassuring to see that Johann didn't have to leave the house barefoot—he wore the grey woolen jacket and leather boots of all Wehrmacht soldiers. They were frightened when they found out where he was being sent: North Africa. The National Socialists had mistreated and humiliated Johann for two years. Now they needed him, and he had to wear their uniform.

Once again, Johann turned around in the doorway and looked at his family. "I will be back." He climbed into the open truck that stood in front of his house, a few Straubingers in their Wehrmacht army uniforms already in it.

Another two years went by, with Johann now stuck in battle to fight Hitler's war. There wasn't a day when Tilly didn't think of her father or pray for his safe return.

Tilly tiptoed into her parent's bedroom to stand in front of the mirror and look at herself. The nine-year-old girl who had cried every night over her father in the concentration camp had become a fourteen-year-old young woman capable of helping to support her family by working in a grocery store. Her workday had ended and now she had to get ready for an obligatory Hitler Youth event in the evening. She looked at herself in her German Girl's uniform and thought of her father who was now fighting somewhere in Libya. The uniform felt like a betrayal: a dark skirt below the knee and a white blouse with a black scarf knotted over her collar. She tried earlier to braid her brown hair into two braids, just like the other girls who belonged to the League of German Girls. But it wouldn't stay in place; her hair was just too unmanageable. She stroked her skirt with her fingers. If her father could see her now, what would he say? Would he be very disappointed? Her hands began shaking. Tilly hated the uniform that all young girls had to wear now. She couldn't stand that they all looked the same and even more, she hated the events in which they had to appear in their uniforms. It felt like they were mocking her father.

Just last week, someone in the city square had screamed into the microphone that the Soviet soldiers close to the border had surrendered themselves to the Wehrmacht. That a victory over the Soviet Union was within reach.

"How would he know that?" Tilly had whispered to the girl next to her, then went back to being quiet again.

While the others at the city square raised their right hand in a Hitler greeting during Sunday roll call, she felt an icy-cold chill down her back. While they shouted "Heil Hitler," Tilly had to mumble along while thinking about the fact that Hitler and his minions had locked her father in a camp, that her father now had to fight on a different continent and might even have to die.

Hans had seen Tilly in his parent's bedroom and stuck his head in, curious as always. He had put on his dark pants and his light brown shirt. On his left upper warm was a red badge with a swastika.

"Well," he said, "at least these things are new." He grinned at his sister. Tilly sighed. What else could they do? They had to wear these clothes, they had to walk in long marches, they had to listen to speeches about the master Aryan race and that all other people on earth are subhuman. What would it accomplish to tear off their swastika badges? One thing Tilly and Hans agreed on—they didn't want to put their mother in more difficulties.

Elke

In 1942 my mother, Tilly, stopped regular school to start working as an apprentice in a Straubing grocery store to become a qualified sales lady. During the war, she shared her tiny portion with begging people who came in hungry with empty pockets. Frequently, a mother or a wife came into the store crying just after discovering that their son or husband had been killed in action.

Then Tilly would think even more about her father who had been transported to Africa as cannon fodder. She remembered the boys she had played with on Gstütt Island. Many of them did not return. But she forced herself to stay strong. Holding tightly to the store counter with both hands, she told herself, "He is coming home again."

At some point her mother, Maria, received mail from the front: a nurse in the African Infirmary wrote that Johann was badly injured in 1942 at the Battle of El Alamein. Of course, the Nazis had bragged through the wireless that the Desert Fox would crush the British.

In Straubing, people were already whispering behind cupped hands that it might no longer be possible to win the war. That the winters in Russia were merciless and that now the Americans were fighting against them. But they still heard many others answer the question: "Do you want total war?" with a loud screaming "Yes!"

One year before the war ended, when the total war so longed for by the Nazis had arrived in Germany with all of its horrors, all remaining young men and teenagers were drafted. Even though, or maybe because, the Allies had landed in France, the Nazis deployed any available forces to the many different fronts. Among these was my fifteen-year-old uncle, Hans, who was handed a steel helmet and a shotgun and dressed in a grey Wehrmacht uniform.

Hans managed to survive the battles but ended up a prisoner of war. The Russians transported him by cattle car to Stalino, which is now in the Ukraine. That was the last news my family received about Hans for many years.

My mother, Tilly, looked out of the grocery store window and saw swarms of refugees from the east passing by in rags with their few possessions, fleeing from the approaching Red Army. At noon on April 18, 1945, as so often before, she heard the sirens howling and ran out of the store down into the air-raid shelter. Like everyone else, she hoped that the roaring and booming over their heads was just the motors of the German fighter planes. Together they prayed, hoped and cried. But the Americans bombed Straubing, killing over three hundred people. The store was untouched, but in the next days, Tilly watched people pushing hearses and wandering through the wreckage, screaming and crying, searching for their relatives.

Only a few days later, when she left the store and walked over the castle bridge toward home, Tilly heard loud screaming from Hagen. What could be happening there, she asked herself. When she arrived at Gstütt Island, she heard shots. She was startled and ran as fast as she could to get home to her mother. Maria had already heard the rumor: SS men had marched thousands of emaciated, completely exhausted people from the concentration camp in Flossenbürg. Every time they heard a bang, it meant they had shot someone else. An old lady whispered to her that the Moosmühl brook was red with blood and that cadavers were floating in it. A small boy confided to her that he had heard people in Hagen screaming desperately for water.

Two days later, Tilly and Maria were woken up by a loud booming sound. The last delusional National Socialists had blown up the Danube Bridge by the ducal castle so that the US troops would be cut off. That was the day that Maria made the decision to pack everything just in case. They stuffed their silverware, a couple of family photos and a little bit of clothing in a bag. Now it was time to use up the emergency rations: Maria took a crowbar from the tool shed, knelt on the floor and pulled up the floorboard. From the hollow space, Johann's secret hiding spot, she pulled out the bundle of Reichsmark and the old watch. But what kind of tin was this? When Maria and Tilly opened the green tin of tea and found the yellowed flyers, they burst into tears and fell into each other's arms. He had been right about everything. It was right to stand up against the inhumanity of the Nazi regime from the beginning, even if you were severely punished. All the doubts and anger they had sometimes felt towards Johann disappeared. Sometimes the truth requires much more courage than lies.

Two days later, the American tanks rolled across the city square. Straubing was occupied, the war was over and Hitler was dead. Adolf Hitler had only provided people with a false sense of winning the war, had not disclosed what was really happening in the camps and in the end forced youngsters like my uncle Hans to protect the bunker he was hiding in. He could not have cared less of what would happen to the German people. He even said "If the German people die out they alone are responsible. German cities deserve to be destroyed, they are too cowardly, people have forsaken me." The dictator who had indoctrinated the German youth to swear in the name of the Fuehrer to sacrifice their life, chose to stay in his bunker and committed suicide by swallowing a cyanide capsule and shooting himself in the head.

I do not remember my grandmother Maria; I only know her from my family's descriptions of her. She had the kindest heart and a soft and giving nature. That gentle heart gave out at fifty-three, when I was three years old and too young to recall her.

A letter fluttered through the mail slot: Johann had been transferred to the infirmary in Bad Aibling, Germany. Even though he was badly injured, the nurse who had written the letter had been told to pass on the news that he would be coming home soon. It would take another three months—three months when Maria and Tilly wondered daily how to best break the news to Johann that Hans had been captured by the Russians and was now a prisoner of war.

From the store, Tilly watched young American men chewing their gum, cigarettes dangling nonchalantly from their lips as they strolled in their uniforms. One of them winked at her through the window. Tilly smiled for the first time in weeks. She thought their crew cuts made them look charming.

Then she remembered how her grandmother Lucia had prophesied that Tilly would one day have a daughter who would be separated from her by an ocean. Let us wait and see what will happen, Tilly thought to herself.

The US soldier smiled back.

Family photo when Johann was conscripted into the German army and sent to fight in the battle of El Alamein where he was wounded. From left to right: My mother Tilly, my grandmother Maria, my uncles Erwin and Hans. In the back middle my grandfather Johann

Chapter 5

Shots, threats and cigarette butts

Alex, Wieluń, Poland, 1939–1940

Alexander Michalowicz came from a well-off and educated Jewish family. He and his five siblings grew up surrounded by farmland, close to the Polish city of Wieluń. From the family home, they looked out over wheat fields ripening in the summer sun and orchards full of cherries, apples and peaches. His father, Arye, oversaw the trade from the fruits of the expansive lands they owned. The family had been industrious for generations and was used to a wealthy standard of living. Alex and his siblings went to the best schools in the neighborhood and his grades were so high that his parents decided that he should study law one day. Alex thought this would be a good choice for him, as he saw himself as a good judge of character and he knew how to differentiate right from wrong. But he liked to dream of being a cantor, too, as singing pleased him so much. He was not yet fourteen and full of ideas for his promising future. When he looked over the expanse of the wheat, he had no idea that he would never get the chance to realize any of his dreams.

The last day of August in the year 1939 was sunny. With his father and his brothers, Alex had harvested the wheat weeks before, so that only stubble could be seen in the fields. Finally, he would have time for other things—for swimming, reading and his beloved German shepherds.

That afternoon, he and his brothers biked to a nearby pond. They bet on who could hold their breath under the water the longest, and who could swim to the other side and back the fastest. As always, his older brothers won. In their wet underpants, they then cycled back over the bumpy path, calling out that the first to reach home would be the winner. Alex was the last to reach the farmhouse, but he didn't mind.

With its red-tiled roof, dark green window posts and spacious verandah, his parents' house looked inviting. Some farmers lived in thrown-together wooden shacks with leaky roofs, but the house that belonged to Alex's family was made of bricks painted white, with a large driveway, a wooden shed for wheat storage, a dog kennel and a small garden bower where his mother sometimes invited her friends over for coffee. His mother had planted a small bed of herbs right in front of the kitchen window. Just a few weeks ago, she had picked off the last tomatoes of the summer. His sisters took care of the flowers, sometimes snipping them to place in a vase for the dining room table. At that moment, Alex's youngest sister was watering the chrysanthemums.

As his brothers leaned their bikes against the stone steps leading to the open green front door, he heard his mother calling. "Are you all here? The food is ready."

Alex biked to the dog kennel at full speed, where three German shepherds pressed their front legs up high against the cage. They barked and panted, their tongues lolling. Alex quickly checked that they had enough water in their bowls. It was so hot that his clothes had dried completely on the bike ride. "I will come and see you later," he said, scratching one behind the ear.

For supper, his mother had made lamb with eggplant, cauliflower and potatoes. She had sprinkled finely snipped basil from her herb garden over everything. She placed the gigantic porcelain platter in the middle of the long table and soon the only sounds were the clattering of plates and cutlery. Juice was poured, salt and water shared, the ladle passed. His younger sister, Hanna, whispered something in his sister Leah's ear that made her laugh and get the hiccups.

One of his older brothers picked at his food with his fork. "What is up with you?" his mother asked.

"I just don't like cauliflower," he sighed.

His father interrupted him. "You will eat what is on the table. Your mother spent an hour cooking this." With his head lowered, his brother cut the cauliflower into pieces with his knife, buried the small pieces within the potato and the eggplant and swallowed them without saying another word.

"Today at the marketplace," Father said, "more and more people were adding their name to the lists."

Mother looked up from her plate, put down her spoon and asked, "What lists do you mean?"

"For the war," he answered in a clipped tone and brought his fork with the buttered potato to his mouth.

Hanna, who had just taken Leah's hair ribbon from her hand and hidden it behind her back, was suddenly quiet.

Leah, the youngest of the family, leaned against the table with her mouth open. The oldest brother let the fork with eggplant and a small piece of cauliflower fall back on his plate. The other put his glass of juice quietly back on the table. Alex looked up. It had gotten very quiet.

"Now it won't be too long," said Father, as he chewed on the potato.

"But," Mother said hastily, "you don't have to be scared. This has nothing to do with us." She looked around the circle and saw her six children more subdued than she had ever seen them.

"The war will come, that is clear," said Father, "but your mother is right. The war will take place near the borders or in the big cities, not here."

"Adam," one of his older brothers murmured. "Adam has already signed up."

"Adam is twenty-one," his father interrupted him. "And also, Adam is not Jewish."

Alex knew Adam. He was a boy from their village who was the same age as his eldest brother. Only last week, he had been to the pond with them. Alex looked at his oldest brother, who was getting ready to say something.

Just then, Leah, feeling the rising tension in the room, started to cry. Her mother stroked her hair tenderly, while Hanna took her hand and squeezed it. "It will be okay," she whispered in her ear, "I'll read to you later when we are done eating."

"But I ..." his oldest brother stammered.

"No buts. You know perfectly well how the Poles have treated us in the last several years. You know that I can only bargain with a few of them now and how very few will buy wheat from me. How they stare at us sometimes in the city.

At the marketplace, only a few people will buy apples and peaches from me, or they try to negotiate lower prices. I don't want one of you to risk your life for this." Father leaned forward to look his eldest son in the eyes. "Do you understand me? War might come, but you will not be signed to any list."

With that, the discussion was over. The girls helped their mother carry the dishes into the kitchen to wash and dry them. Father lit his cigar on the verandah and all the brothers went to their rooms to study, except for Alex.

Alex was the first to get up from the table. He picked up the dog leashes and the key to the kennel. He ran to the dog kennel and unlocked it. The three shepherds barked with excitement but obeyed instantly when he said, "Quiet!" and "Sit." He stroked their heads and snapped the leash hooks on their collars. Then they got moving, away from the farmyard and along a path through the fields. From one of the gnarled trees along the way, Alex snagged himself a red apple and bit into it, holding the leashes in the other hand.

"Come, Luka, let's go," he said, clicking his tongue. His oldest dog, Luka, had trouble keeping up with the two younger dogs.

"Luka, off we go," he carefully patted the dog on the back of the leg that seemed to be dragging. I wonder how much longer this will go well, he thought. Luka was almost as old as he was, almost fourteen. As a child, Alex had often tied Luka to his bike and let the dog pull him around the yard. Each time he sat at the table, he swiped a piece of food and hid it in his pocket so he could give Luka a treat. Even now he had some potato in his pocket that he stuffed into Luka's mouth. His father always reminded him that dogs were there to protect the house. They were working animals and shouldn't be spoiled. But Luka was not a working animal for Alex.

Once, when he was younger and coming home alone from school, two neighborhood boys ambushed him on the small path from the little forest close to their house. The farm boys had been furious because Alex had a new school satchel and new shoes. Since Alex was so thin, they weren't worried about him fighting back. They postured in front of him before grabbing his satchel, throwing it in the mud and stomping on his shoes. They laughed and yelled at him. Alex was scared stiff, not moving a muscle.

The bigger of the two slapped Alex hard across the face and hissed at him. "Jewish pig!"

Alex tried to catch his breath, and then he heard it in the distance: barking, coming closer, in a hurry. The farm boys turned around as a small cloud of dust moved towards them along the field path. Luka stormed in between them, clamping his jaws around the leg of one of the two. When he let go, he barked viciously, baring his teeth. That was enough for the bigger one, who took off as fast as he could. He left his younger companion behind, screaming and holding his leg until he finally limped away. After that afternoon, they had left Alex alone.

The sun was low in the sky now, blanketing the stubble field with rose-colored light. In the distance, Alex heard the bell of the St. Joseph Church in Wieluń. When he squinted, he could see both spire towers. "Soooo," he said in a deep voice. "We need to turn around." He pulled lightly on the leash. The three dogs understood immediately and turned to walk back home along the field path. His mother had already turned the light on in the living room. His brothers still brooded over their homework as their father smoked and leafed through the newspaper on the verandah. Alex opened the dog kennel and let the animals in. While the other two shepherds immediately ran to the water bowls and started lapping at them, Luka stayed with him and leaned against his knee. Alex patted him on the back. “Good night,” he whispered.

All the children had their own rooms except Leah, who still slept with her parents. Alex’s room had a fireplace with green tiles, a small bookshelf, a desk with a globe, a bed with an embroidered cover and a nightstand. On the nightstand was a songbook that he sometimes used when singing with his mother. After he had washed his face, scrubbed his hands and brushed his teeth, he slipped under the light cotton blanket into bed. The covers smelled like soap and a little bit like summer. A maid had soaked it in the tub that morning and then hung it up on a line in the fruit orchard. Alex put his nose close to it and breathed in deeply—it smelled like apple blossoms and grass. At least that is what he imagined.

It was now dark out. He heard his brother grumbling, most likely over some math homework, and the annoying whine of a mosquito buzzing directly above his head. Alex turned on his side, pulled the blanket over his ears and tried to sleep.

But he could still hear the buzzing and it was getting louder. He flapped his hand around his head, half asleep. A whole swarm of mosquitos must have come into his room through the open window. He crawled deeper under the duvet and covered his ears.

But the buzzing became louder and louder. Now there was also a droning, a roaring and a jingling sound. Alex threw the duvet off. The small lamp on the ceiling of his room with its many glass crystals was shaking, which he realized was the source of the jingling. The whole room seemed to be shaking and he jumped up. Something roared and rattled and again he put his hands over his ears. What could it be? Outside, the dogs were barking and howling, but they could only be heard when the roaring stopped briefly. Then a loud bang made Alex almost fall over backwards. Suddenly, it was bright in his room and he ran to the window. On the horizon, behind his father's orchard, it was as bright as day even though it was still night.

The buzzing started again, becoming louder and closer. He couldn't bear it anymore. Alex burst out of his room and his brothers were already running towards him. His sisters were screaming and crying, their mother pressing Leah against her as she tried to get down the stairs.

The front door was wide open. Their father stood looking out. Motionless, his mouth open, he clutched the door frame.

"That … that is Wieluń," he stammered.

"What are you saying?" his oldest brother shouted, directly beside him. The buzzing and rattling sound was again so loud nothing else could be heard. His brother pressed the palms of his hands over his ears.

"Wieluń is burning," screamed his mother, pointing outside. Again, a crash and Alex believed the house was collapsing. A giant fireball rose above the orchard in the night sky.

"They are bombing the city," said Father. Whirling around, he shrieked, "Into the basement!"

Alex and Hanna grabbed each other's hands, pushing forward and tugging each other as they ran down the stone steps to the vaulted cellar below. His father slammed the door behind him and fumbled on a shelf for a matchstick and a candle. Over their heads, they heard a buzzing that became a shrill howl and ended in a deafening bang.

"Mother, mother, what is that?" cried Leah, huddled under her mother's protective arm.

"Those are airplanes," said her mother and began to cry. They sat close to one another in the corner of the cellar, their backs against the stone wall. Alex's oldest brother put his head between his bent knees and seemed to be saying something silently to himself, perhaps a prayer. Another brother closed his eyes, leaning his head back against the wall.

Hanna held Alex's hand, and each time the buzzing sound came closer, she squeezed it tighter. Just like always, thought Alex. As a little girl, Hanna had often slipped into his room when she was scared, crawling under his blanket and holding his hand. They had imagined that they were driving ghosts away. Hanna was just one year younger than Alex and they walked the same path to school, had the same friends and similar dreams. Hanna had preferred playing with Alex rather than with Leah, who was so much younger. And Alex felt more comfortable in Hanna's room than with his older brothers. He could sing out of the songbook with her. He even liked helping her with her work on the flowerbeds.

Now, at fourteen, Alex was already a young man. Hanna was thirteen, almost a young lady, but they still clung to each other as they had when they were children.

Dust trickled down on them. Each time the crashing came, they held on tight and started crying again. Only their father stared at the small candle in front of him. He didn't cry. His eyes were wide open, and his skin was pale. "Anna," Alex mumbled to himself.

Anna was Father's sister. She owned a fabric shop in the middle of the town and lived in a beautiful apartment above it. From her windows, Alex had watched the hustle and bustle of the streets for hours while Hanna was allowed to trim silk and lace with Anna. Alex could not think of her at this moment. He could only think of Luka and how scared he must be in the dog kennel. If Alex had his way, he would have run out of the basement to get him, but his father would never have permitted it.

They held their ears closed as the beams above them creaked and the sky roared.

Finally, there was silence, broken only by Leah's whimpering and the sobs of his mother. How long it took for Father to stand up with the candle in his hand, walk up the stairs, open the door and stagger outside, Alex was never able to remember.

At some point, they all stood on the verandah. It was daytime. The sun was up, the birds chirped in the orchards, and a gigantic dark cloud hung over Wieluń. Even by their front door the air smelled burnt. They could barely breathe, each breath stinging. Alex tore himself from Hanna's grip and ran to the dog kennel where the dogs crouched in a corner. Luka came to him and Alex whispered endearing words, touching him through the fence.

Over the radio, they heard that Hitler had attacked Poland. There would be war now. In the course of the next few hours, people covered with dust dragged themselves past their house along the field paths, their clothing torn, their eyes vacant. The children cried and screamed. His mother and sisters got all the food they could find in the house and pressed it into the hands of people who took it wordlessly and kept walking.

Alex's father, who had been listening to the radio all morning, stood by the garden fence and asked everyone who went by where they were from, and if they knew the fabric store that belonged to his sister. They only stared down at the path and shook their heads.

Elke

On September 1, 1939, the German air force leveled a city with no military significance whatsoever. Over one thousand people were burned, suffocated, crushed or buried. One of them was Alex's Aunt Anna, whose house had been hit. That evening, the only things left standing among the heap of rubble were the towers of St. Joseph Church. The Second World War had begun. A day later, the German Army moved in and occupied the city.

Soon, Jewish people were forced into ghettos, required to provide compulsory labor or were shot, their houses taken. My father's family tried to protect themselves against this. His father, Arye, was an important merchant in the area. He knew other influential people and had the financial ability to pay some of them off in order to protect his family, and so they were able to stay in their home. They might have been in a good situation then, but it would change dramatically very soon. For the time being, Alex and his brothers built a wooden fence around their yard. The dogs were left outside every evening so they could announce any intruders. Arye, Alex and his brothers divided the night into shifts and took turns creeping from window to window. But all this vigilance failed.

On July 25, 1940, the life of my father, Alex, my grandfather, Arye, my Aunt Hanna and my whole family's life, changed forever.

Fog hung over the wheat fields. It had rained all night and large puddles had formed in the entrance of the farmyard. Arye and his sons wanted to harvest more apples that day and distribute them that afternoon. The woven baskets were already waiting on the steps.

Arye sat at the kitchen table sipping a cup of steaming coffee. Suddenly he heard the dogs barking on high alert. He put his cup to the side, grabbed the hammer he had kept handy for the past year, and ran to the door. Just as he opened it, there was a loud bang. The fence had collapsed, and a black limousine was driving over the wooden slats, with two others following behind. As if it were natural for a limousine to drive over a fence, the limousines glided into the driveway. The first one stopped right in front of the entrance. A man with a black jacket and dark cap cranked the car window down.

"Keep your dogs away," he commanded.

The shepherds growled and barked at him. The whole family had assembled after hearing the commotion. The sisters clung to their mother, who was holding their father's arm with one hand, holding him back. The brothers stood next to their father.

"I am telling you for the last time—keep your dogs away," roared the voice from the car.

Alex slipped away from his brothers and his father and crept down the stairs.

"Alex, come back," his mother whispered. But Alex could think only of his dog.

"Luka," he said hesitantly, "Luka, come back." But Luka didn't listen, and barked even louder, leaning against the driver's door with his front paws. The man with the black cap looked the dog in the eyes.

"Luka," called Alex. But Luka kept barking as he never had before. The man hissed something to the other man in the passenger seat. Then he lifted his right hand and Alex saw the revolver. He squeezed the trigger and shot Luka right between the eyes. The dog howled, shuddered briefly and then fell to the ground. Blood ran down the driver's door. The crows in the nearby trees, startled by the bang, flew up, screeching loudly. His sisters started crying.

"Luka," Alex screamed, running towards the lifeless body.

"Alex, stay here," his father called after him. But Alex was already kneeling by his childhood friend.

"No, Luka, don't die," Alex whispered, patting him gently on the stomach. But Luka never moved again.

The man opened the driver's door and stepped over Luka with his polished boots. Alex looked up. The man grinned down at him, still holding the revolver in his right hand. He aimed at the other dog that came running up, then turned swiftly on his heel, pointed the revolver at the third dog and shot him, too.

Tears ran down Alex's cheeks. He stood up and started screaming: "Why did you do that? They didn't do anything to you! What kind of a beast are you?"

The man with the long black coat and the cap stared at him. He hadn't expected this. He briskly marched towards Alex, grabbed his arm, bent it behind his back and held it there with one hand while he pushed his head forward with the other. "Just be grateful that I haven't picked you off, as well," he murmured. Alex could feel his breath on the back of his neck. The man loosened his grip and pushed him forward. Alex fell on the ground, landing next to his dead dog.

One at a time, the doors of the black limousines opened, and a dozen dark-clothed men climbed out. Some leaned against the car. Others looked around, trampling on the herb garden and the colorful flowerbeds. They strutted onto the verandah, throwing a vase and Arye's chair down the steps.

The leader lit a cigarette. With icy grey eyes, he glanced at the family standing motionless by the front door. He went past Alex, swung himself up the stairs and stood as imposingly as possible in front of Arye. He blew the smoke from the cigarette into his face.

"Jew," he hissed. "You don't know me yet, but that doesn't matter. You will get to know me."

Arye met his gaze. He tried to stay calm, especially since he still felt the grip of his wife holding him back.

"You are an influential Jew," said the man, grinning coldly. "You should be very grateful. Otherwise I would have shot you, too. You've influential friends." He raised one of his eyebrows. He turned on his heels and jumped down the stairs to the ground. He looked back at them and then turned his gaze up to the large windows and balcony. "You have it nice here," he said, and laughed out loud.

He stopped where Alex sat in a state of shock with Luka. The man grabbed him under the armpits and pulled him up. With a tight grip, he turned Alex's palm upward and pressed his cigarette against it. Alex cried out and simultaneously heard his mother scream, "No, no." Alex tried to pull his hand away, but the man's grip was so tight he couldn't even move it by a millimeter. It smelled like burnt meat. Suddenly his hand felt terribly cold, then the pain shot through his body. From within the black ash, blood oozed from his palm.

The man shoved him to the side, climbed up the stairs again, grabbed Hanna by the arm and ripped her away from her mother and down the stairs. He pulled his revolver from its halter and pressed it against Hanna's forehead. She closed her eyes and whimpered. He pulled her head even farther back by her long dark hair. His mother ran down the stairs, fell on her knees and begged him, "No, not my child. Take me. Take me!" The man laughed loudly and pushed Hanna against the stairs. He kicked her with his heavy boots. Hanna stayed completely still.

As if he had given a command, all the black-clothed men came running back to the limousines. Before they drove away, the leader shouted from his window, "You will soon have a new home."

They raced over the wooden fence boards, down the field path and disappeared in a cloud of dust.

Chapter 6

Train rides—leaving family, belongings and hope behind

Alex, 1940–1945

THE NEXT DAY, THE SS CAME FOR ALEX'S FAMILY.

The large truck rolled over the demolished fence in the morning. The officer in charge pounded on the door, shouting that everyone was allowed only one suitcase. Mother stuffed a warm fleece blanket, the children's good leather shoes, pearls from her mother and a few banknotes into her big travel bag. Father opened the chest under his bed and shoved jewelry and money into his suit pockets. He had heard that everything would be taken away in the camps, but he had no intention of going to one. Alex packed his winter coat, his thick shoes and his songbook.

After a few minutes, the family arrived at the entrance with their suitcases. They were told to climb into the truck, where another family already cowered in a corner. The officer, who clearly remembered that Alex had called him a beast, held him back until everyone had boarded—then gave him a hard shove, smashing his head against the wooden bench where the others were already sitting. Blood ran down his face. Then the truck roared to life and bumped over the fallen wooden fence posts. Alex pulled himself up to look out of the rear of the truck and saw the home of his parents for the last time in his life.

"Where are they taking us?" Hanna asked, tears running down her cheeks.

Mother held her index finger against her lips, "Shhh." An SS man with a revolver sat in between them, observing every movement. No one said another word. The truck raced over field paths. They were thrown back and forth so much Alex almost threw up. If I stand up quickly and jump down, I could escape, Alex thought. But here, in the wide-open fields, it would be easy for the guard to shoot him.

He would have to wait until they reached the forest, Alex decided. He would leave his suitcase. Then he could hide in the woods overnight and try to make it home the next day. From there, he could call the police or his uncle who lived in Wieluń. He would get some help. Just as he was thinking this, the truck stopped with a jerk. They had arrived at a railway station.

An old locomotive engine steamed and hissed. A guard tore the tailgate open and bellowed, "*Raus*! Everyone out!" One after the other, they climbed out of the truck. The station was full of people of all ages: from elderly people with walking sticks to little children with dolls or stuffed animals and women holding infants in their arms. Everyone had a suitcase.

Alex heard whimpering and whispering under the continuous shouting of the SS men and the barking of their dogs. Dogs like Luka, but nothing like him—they looked vicious and mean.

"Let's go," screamed the guard and made a motion for them to hurry up. He pushed Alex's father and his mother, who held hands with Hanna and Leah, through the crowd. A different guard pulled both his brothers to the track and barked at Alex, "You, get over here too."

Now, thought Alex, now is my last chance to run. But then the guard might shoot him and hit other people.

"Stay together," he heard his father say, "I'll come and get you."

Alex looked at line after line of cattle cars with desperate people being pushed into them. The SS men stood by the tracks and forced children and women and into the cattle cars. It was pitch black and smelled like excrement and urine. In the darkness, Alex could hear infants and children crying and grown-ups whispering.

"In with you," the SS man on the platform roared as he shoved an elderly man so brutally the man fell to the ground. The SS man laughed and kicked him in the ribs. The man was slight and frail and doubled over in pain. His wife, who had already been shoved into the train, jumped out and threw herself over her husband. The SS man instantly pulled out his revolver and shot them both. There was an outcry in the car and then it became deadly still.

"Did you see that?" an SS man yelled through the opening. "That is what happens to anyone who doesn't listen." Nobody said anything. The SS man shoved the door closed and latched it from the outside.

The train began to rattle and hiss and then started moving. They stood still, holding each other up. They leaned on each other, packed like sardines, for hours.

Alex could only tell where people were standing by their voices. He tried to move his nose closer to an opening in the wall of the train to breathe some fresh air. He also tried to look through the slit so that he might be able to recognize where they were going.

Eventually the train stopped. They had arrived at the destination the SS commandant had described as their new home. Alex's mother and sisters were shoved to one side, while Alex and his brothers were pushed to the other. Their belongings were taken, labeled with chalk and placed in the middle. They were told that they would be able to get them back later. An SS man roared at Alex's group, "Stand in a line, one after the other!"

After a guard pulled an old man and a small boy out of the row, Alex's brother turned around and whispered to him, "Try to look bigger, and say that you are older, or they'll kill you."

One after the other, they approached a table manned by a grim-looking SS guard, who would look up from his typewriter to either say, "Keep going," or nod to the guard beside him. Whenever he nodded, the guard would grab that person and push him towards the old man and the young boy. "They are weeding out the weaker ones," a man behind Alex said. "They want to know you are capable of work."

Alex walked on his toes to appear bigger. At one point, he looked to the left and saw that it was his mother's turn to go up to the table on the women's side. The SS guard looked up and said something that Alex couldn't hear. At least he didn't nod, thought Alex. His mother looked over to him and his brothers. Her eyes glistened strangely—that much he could tell from the distance. She pressed her lips together and tried to smile. Then she was pushed forward along with Leah and Hanna. She turned around one last time and waved at Alex. The three disappeared behind the many other women who were shoved forward by the SS guards.

It was almost Alex's turn. Two guards with German shepherds pushed him forward. As he reached the table, he noticed a rock by his feet and stood on it.

"Age?" the officer asked.

"Eighteen," Alex said, surprised by how easily the lie slipped from his lips.

The man looked up to inspect him. "Good," he said. "Keep going."

He was herded away to a group of men he had never met. Beside him, a young man with wide-open eyes stared at the ground and rocked back and forth apathetically. Behind him, a man almost as old as Alex's father was crying. Where was his father? Where were his brothers? Alex looked around. He saw many faces, young and old, distraught, tear-stained and somber, but he couldn't find his father. He'd assumed that his father and brothers would remain in the same group as him.

Alex looked at the groups that were being formed, snarled at by dogs and laughed at by guards. Men with grey hair clutched canes and small boys whimpered. He was relieved; neither his father nor his brothers were in that group. Alex turned around and stood up on his toes again to look past the figures crowding around him to find his father and his brothers.

He had no idea that he would never see them again.

Alex had saved himself from death by lying about his age. Now he had to live alongside men and work for more than twelve hours a day in unspeakable camp conditions.

His head had been shaved, his clothes and all his possessions were taken away; only a pair of striped pajamas and a pair of clogs were given to him to wear. A tattoo was placed on his left arm with which he was now to be identified. His name was lost altogether. It was best to forget he was only fifteen and worked as hard as any of these men who had to help build the camp. The SS men seemed to get diabolical pleasure from watching people set up their own squalid sleeping barracks and building the gas chambers between the earth walls. During the nights, thoroughly exhausted on his wooden bed in the barracks, the darkness interrupted only by the watchtower search lights, he thought of his soft bed at home. They slept on wooden slats—there was no mattress or sheets, no pillow. But he could take off his pants and roll them together behind his head to form a head rest. He struggled to remember how it had smelled like apple blossoms in the summer and how the soft blankets kept him warm in winter.

When he had to stand in line in snow, rain or wind in the evening waiting for his meal of watery soup, he tried to remember the fresh vegetables and herbs in his mother's garden and the tender meat she prepared for the family.

For the early morning roll call, when it was still dark, he imagined sitting at the table with his parents and siblings, laughing or even fighting, recalling the warmth he had always felt with them, no matter what. That he would not see them again was unfathomable. The thought of reuniting with them kept his mind believing in all that's good in humanity and kept him alive.

Daily he watched people being forced with rifle butts and whips, people dying and being dumped somewhere on top of each other. He lived cramped—lice and all sorts of disease and infections invaded the camp, with many people dying every day just from that. Nevertheless, Alex lived in fear of being selected for transport, which had torn him away from all he loved.

Alex was transported several times to different camps. He did not know what happened to his siblings or parents and was alone in an unpredictable hostile world. He dreaded that the next destination would even be worse than the one before. He was particularly horrified to stand with a hundred people in a closed cattle car, exhausted, hungry and anxious, not even being able to sit, one bucket to relieve yourself in. These trips culminated in the arrival at another camp with despicable horrors.

One of the concentration camps he was moved to was Mauthausen in Austria. In a fortress that looked like an old castle, he was forced to work in a stone quarry. The prisoners pounded the granite out of the cliffs that the Führer needed for his latest monumental building projects.

As Alex broke up rocks in the blazing sun, in what was known as the Knochenmuehle—the "bone crusher"—it wasn't unusual for someone to drop dead from exhaustion. It was what the Nazis wanted: elimination through work. But no matter how hungry Alex was or how he despised the thin soup and grey bread or how emaciated he became, he always told himself: "I will see my family again."

In the evenings, in the barracks, the prisoners talked about their favorite foods, from a juicy roast to a savory vegetable casserole. Those who still had a bit of energy left would demonstrate how they would eat at a luxuriously appointed table. With growling and bloated stomachs, they fell asleep each night only to be awakened by the SS men to be tormented and humiliated a few hours later. If they weren't woken during the night, they knew that the morning roll call would be worse than usual. Barefoot or with their feet wrapped in rags, they stood in the ice and snow. It was still pitch black and it wasn't unusual for an SS man to whip a stick against their shins or stomachs. To be able to use the toilet in the morning without being disturbed, to brush their teeth and wash—it was all that the people who could still get out of their barracks wanted to do in the morning. Instead, they were screamed at and herded to roll call before waiting, often in vain, at the few dirty wooden outhouses.

As soon as it was light, they would see it: the smoke rising above the crematoriums.

Every day, they dragged heavy stone blocks down a flight of crooked stairs that connected the stone quarry to the concentration camp. Whoever fell was shot.

Alex exchanged stories with the young man who lay next to him in the barracks. They told each other things about their families, their friends, their rooms and what they used to enjoy doing.

Alex told him about the little pond and about Luka. One evening, he spoke about the family of Rachel, a girl he was sweet on, who had been taken away by train as well. He didn't know where.

The young man replied, "You will see her again, look forward to that. When everything here is done."

The next morning, the young man lost his strength. He dropped his granite boulder and tumbled down the rickety stairs.

Alex scrambled close to him to help him up, hoping that nobody had noticed the fall. But the guard was faster and shot the young man in front of everyone, his blood splattering over Alex's striped clothing and his face. The corpse was thrown into a pit like garbage and quickly buried in a heap of others.

That evening, Alex lay on the wooden bunk in the barracks. He heard whimpering, crying, the creaking of the beds, the coughing and heavy breathing of those who were ill, and occasionally, the screaming of people who had been driven crazy or who had awakened from a nightmare. The air in the barracks smelled like sweat, excrement, urine and vomit, overlaid with an unmistakable odor of rot. Alex closed his eyes, and his mind went to the friend he had lost today. Suddenly, he heard a crack in his mouth. He could taste blood—his first tooth had fallen out.

At that moment, he doubted he could survive Mauthausen. He feared he would choke in the gas chambers, collapse in the quarry or be shot by an SS man for any reason at all. But he was later transferred to the Flossenbürg concentration camp.

In Flossenbürg, Alex also had to hammer out stones in a quarry and excavate clay for the brickyard. Others had to manufacture components for the German Air Force. He lived, like so many others, in long barracks that were attached to one another. From stone watchtowers, the SS controlled the mass of emaciated figures who dragged themselves to roll call in the mornings and evenings. They were herded into the stone quarry and kept barely alive with a daily piece of bread.

Alex tried to hold his head up straight and to look at the tops of the trees around the camp. He remembered what it felt like to climb into an apple tree with his brothers, how they had built a small treehouse up high, and the taste of a fresh, juicy apple on his tongue.

Alex was transported again, even before the Nazis began to cover their tracks early in 1945. They were desperately trying to hide one of the greatest crimes ever perpetrated against humanity. In order to hide the debasing conditions and treatment that people confined in concentration camps had to endure, the Nazis began to shoot, gas and quickly bury the inmates. The few who could stand on their own legs were forced on long death marches across the country.

But Alex was moved to Ganacker, a satellite camp of Flossenbürg, close to Landau, which was established a few months before the end of the war. Situated in the vicinity of a military airbase, the inmates lived in holes in the ground in conditions that made them long to be in another camp. At least in barracks they had a roof over their heads and relatively dry feet at night. Now, they crouched for hours in muddy, soggy pits in the ground.

Alex's tattered and flea-infested striped clothes were clammy, the material stiff with cold. It had been a long time since he felt warm. Every morning, he felt his toes and squeezed them.

Alex was lucky. The man who slept beside him in the pit had his toes frozen off. He tried to hide that he was shaking with chills and fever and that the flesh of his toes had started to rot. But as he hobbled along, the guards stopped him. The man pulled himself upright, but the SS men didn't tolerate any appearance of weakness. They shot him in the head. His blood-covered corpse, eyes wide open, stayed there on the ground for two days until the guards finally ordered the other prisoners to drag him away and throw him into the pit for the dead.

Every morning, Alex climbed out of his hole in the ground, wondering who had survived the night. He lined up with the others to receive his food: a few sips of watery soup. He stared at the ground so that he wouldn't attract the attention of the SS men. When the man in front of him took a step, he followed.

One day, something felt different. He squinted at the SS man walking back and forth along the line. He knew the man and had often seen him around. Today, he seemed nervous. Then another SS man walked up and they held a whispered conversation. To Alex, it didn't look like they were planning to meet for a card game later or even making plans to humiliate or shoot someone. They looked at each other solemnly and spoke quietly.

No "Heil Hitler."

Alex shuffled another step and watched them. One man lowered his head and held his forehead. The other pressed his lips together. Could he have tears in his eyes? Both of them turned around and went away.

For the rest of this day, Alex heard more shots than usual. He had stopped counting them, but it was more, for sure. When, after hours of backbreaking labor, they were forced back into their pits, the group seemed smaller. He could see that the pit next to his was empty.

Before he could climb into his muddy hole, he heard one of the SS men screaming, "Pack your things, whatever you have. Tomorrow you will be transferred to a new camp." What was he supposed to pack up? He had nothing left. His striped rags were his only possession.

When it was fully dark, someone hissed, "Hey, hey!"

Alex, who had just found an almost tolerable position to sleep in, sat up unwillingly. "What?" he whispered.

Another prisoner looked down into his dirt hole. "They want to take us away on a train tomorrow," he whispered.

"Where?" Alex asked.

"I am not sure. All I know is that we will be gone from here." The man seemed pleased.

"Where did you hear the news about a train?"

"I overheard them talking."

When a dog began barking, the man rushed back to his dirt hole.

Alex was now wide awake. No, they wouldn't go to the trouble of bringing us to another camp, he thought. They would gas or shoot us.

He thought of the SS men that morning. What could make such people cry? Only their own defeat. Perhaps the war was lost already? Was another army on the way towards them?

Alex remembered the cattle trains that had carried his family away from home. What he would have given to get away, to hide.

He made his decision: "I won't be picked up tomorrow," he whispered.

Beside him, he heard the others wheezing and coughing. A little further away, he could hear a dog barking and a few guards talking. It had become quieter during the last few weeks. Only a little while ago, the SS men would have been laughing and hollering. Still, he would have to wait until most of them went back to their barracks.

It was around eight o'clock at night, but at this time of the year, it was pitch black. The most important thing was to get out of the dirt hole. It was clear that he would not be able to escape from the camp. He would have to find a place where they would never expect a living soul to be—with the dead. He knew the pit filled with the corpses. There, he could hide. There, no one would find him.

After a moment, he shook his head. I can't hide among the dead. I won't be able to do it, he thought.

For many minutes, Alex just sat there, rocking back and forth. He thought of his mother, and tried to remember how she laughed, how she smelled, how it felt when she stroked his hair, how warm her skin felt when she hugged him. He saw his sister Hanna in front of him, how she played the piano. He imagined that he could hear his father bantering with his brothers on the verandah.

From his hole in the ground he could hear the SS men inside their accommodation. They wouldn't be coming out into the cold for some time.

This was his chance. If he did not want to be picked up, he had to go.

Slowly, Alex crawled out of his hole. He walked on his toes through the mud, careful not to splash in a puddle or step on a creaky branch. In the dirt holes, nobody was moving. He stopped and listened. He could hear nothing, no dogs, no guards. He kept going.

I can make it, he told himself. Step after step, he came closer to the pit of corpses, the place he had always tried to avoid. Now he could smell it: the stench of decay permeating the air. Alex started gagging. He stopped and bent forward, but his stomach was empty. There was nothing to vomit.

Keep going. There is no other way, Alex told himself. He held his sleeve over his mouth and his nose.

Even in the dark, he could recognize the blue and white striped clothing, the bony hands, the skulls and scratched-up feet. Alex slid down the earth wall and stayed in a couched position. Again, he listened. But all was quiet. Before he moved the first stiffened corpse to the side, he paused briefly.

"I will never, ever forget you," he said, and touched the sleeve of one of the bodies. He closed his eyes and shoved the corpse to the side with both hands. When he opened his eyes, he recognized the body lying below him. It was Josef, the young man he had talked to over their watery soups a few days ago. Alex shuddered. Josef's eyes were closed and there was a big black hole in his forehead.

Alex had to continue moving if he didn't want to be picked up for the last transport. As if in a trance, he pushed and shoved until he created a small cave. He slipped inside and pulled a body over the opening. Then he began to shake. Never, not in all these years, had he felt more miserable. This was the end. Again and again he retched, but nothing came up.

"I am so sorry," he whispered, apologizing to the corpses around him. He was not able to cry anymore.

That whole night, he didn't close his eyes, but cowered in the cave, surrounded by corpses. He listened carefully for any sound, an SS man walking around or a dog sniffling. But the night was quiet. Only the wind whistled through the mountains of dead bodies, and sometimes it sounded as if they were quietly whimpering. But Alex no longer experienced any fear. These were his friends and they were protecting him.

When dawn came, he heard screaming, whistling and shots far away. It had been a cold night, and he massaged his toes. Again and again he heard screaming, but slowly, the sounds seemed to retreat. It became quieter and quieter, until he suddenly couldn't hear anything. Yet he stayed where he was. He had to be patient.

When it stayed quiet, he wondered if they could have moved the whole camp and whether the guards were still there. He peeked out from between the legs of one of the corpses. There were no watchmen on the hills, no dogs. He had to get out of there.

Alex scrambled out from among the dead. He left the camp and stumbled into the chaotic conditions that surrounded it during the last weeks of the war. He moved as fast as he could, along field paths and through small patches of forest. He remembered joking around with his brothers and chasing them once upon a time in a place very similar. The memory gave him strength.

He kept going until he stood in front of a field of green wheat that looked just like his father's field. Tears ran down his cheeks. He was back with the living.

With the last bit of strength in his twenty-year-old body, Alex dragged himself to the small farmhouse that stood behind the field and banged on the wooden door with his fist.

He heard steps approaching and the door opened. A rough looking farmer in a hand knitted sweater stood in front of Alex. The farmer's eyes went wide, and he gasped and recoiled in shock, covering his eyes at the emaciated figure clinging to life. "Dear God, how did you manage to get here? We heard rumors, terrible stories, whispers in the village … but we couldn't … it was impossible … we knew what would happen if …" The farmer turned white and he sagged, clutching the doorframe with trembling hands. If any Nazis were in pursuit of this ghost-like creature at his door he would be done for.

His wife, wiping her hands on her apron came to the door to see what was going on. She stumbled in shock at the nightmarish sight. “Holy Jesus, have mercy on us,” she hissed, and with a furtive look around, the farmer and his wife quickly dragged Alex inside. The door slammed shut and Alex leaned against it. He was alive.

Elke

The Pichlhubers were the kind of people my dad had great admiration for throughout his life. Despite all that was done to him by the Nazis, Dad admired these German people who lived by their principles. They brought him into their kitchen, made him a bread soup and gave him something warm to drink. They bathed him and burned his striped clothing in the fireplace. Frau Pichlhuber prepared a room and made a fresh bed for him, and she and her husband led him there and put him to bed. For the first time in years, he was warm again.

That night, Alex felt as if he was lying in his childhood room in his house in Wieluń, and he slept more deeply than he had in five years.

The Pichlhubers hid him for several weeks until the war was over, until his hair grew in again and he gained some weight. Then, after the official liberation by the Allies, they took him to Straubing to the hospital.

Alex had found the right farmers.

For the rest of his life my father became emotional when he tried to advise me on what to look for in people. “Never mind race or religion. There are good people and bad people in every country and wherever you go. Those with integrity are the real gems.”

My father Alex saved himself from the gas chambers by making himself older, saying he was 18 instead of 15. This was the first photos after the war. Alex sits in the front to the right – looking defiant and much younger than the rest.

Chapter 7

From Different Worlds

How Alex Met Tilly

Elke

Like many cities throughout Germany after the war, Straubing had a denazification program through which citizens like my grandfather offered assistance to Jewish refugees. There were many survivors in the area, and Alex, who would become my father, chose to remain in Straubing, which was about the same size as the town of Wieluń, and was also surrounded by wheat fields and farmland. The United Nations Relief and Rehabilitation Administration (UNRRA) provided him with an apartment that had previously been occupied by a Nazi, but Alex needed to find a way to support himself. At the age of twenty, he was still emotionally fifteen. He had lost five years and had no higher education, but he came from a merchant family and knew how to trade. He was also great at making connections—what we today would call networking.

The end of the war saw the creation of a robust black market, which arose out of necessity. There were shortages of items such as sugar, eggs, meat and cigarettes, and my father saw an opportunity to provide one group of people with what they needed by buying it from those who had it. He was always fair to both sides and saw this as a win/win situation. Farmers had sugar made from sugar beets and eggs, both of which merchants and manufacturers required. Dad saw the black market as a way to satisfy both and make a living at the same time, but unlike some others in this trade, he never tried to enrich himself by pitting buyers against sellers.

Because he was honest, he was trusted by his clients, although there was certainly a risk in what he was doing. The black market was, after all, not legal, but Dad actually enjoyed the risk, so long as it wasn't foolish and no one got hurt.

Johann, the man who would become my grandfather, was also totally honest and trustworthy. He was drawn to my dad, and vice versa. He liked and helped Alex, and to show his appreciation, my dad took a gift of sugar to his house. That's how my dad met my mother, Tilly. She was seventeen at the time and already a skilled businesswoman. When Johann was conscripted into the army, she'd had to leave school to help support the family. My dad could empathize with that and could certainly appreciate the fact that she was pretty and always managed to look great despite the deprivations of the time. She was a flirt, as was my dad, and they both loved to dance. She also loved high heels and nylon stockings, both of which Dad managed to procure for her. And while they had both lost the opportunity to be educated, they had a natural intelligence, an intuition that can't be bought or learned.

The problem, of course, was that they came from different worlds, and in other times they would never have found one another. But these were unusual times. Alex and Tilly began to build a life together, first by flirting with one another, then by talking about building a business together. While trading in the black market, Alex had saved 30,000 Reichsmarks and was smart enough to anticipate that his money might lose its value—which it did, to the tune of 90 percent, as a result of the Currency Reform of 1948, when Reichsmarks were converted to Deutschmarks. So, he bought livestock, which he housed on a nearby farm and used for trading purposes.

In 1950 he was offered the opportunity to establish a delicatessen in the town center, and it was at that point that my dad put the stamp on claiming his new life. My parents got married.

Even though he had not been able to find anyone in his family, and he was smitten with my mother, he would have thought long and hard about marriage to a German woman. At times there was talk of emigration, as most of his post-war friends did just that. But for Alex, who was traumatized so young and so deeply, life in Straubing had become a new normal. He had his name back and a household that ran like clockwork. As long as there was a safe place without the trauma of transport and unbearable uncertainty, life was as usual—a new usual. After a while it was easier to forget that he had really prayed with his father and brothers in the synagogue. Now his name had a new ring: Alexander Michalowicz, Feine Fleisch- und Wurstwaren, fine meats and delicatessen. He was surrounded by ham and pork, the staples of a Bavarian diet, a far cry from the home he lost.

Thinking about his family in Poland, worrying about them, writing to the Red Cross yielded nothing but heartache. Now when he was reminded of the pain of loss, he had a way to detach himself; he could work instead. Surrounded by ham and pork, there was less chance to think of his mother, who kept a kosher home. There was no lock of hair, no photos, no candle sticks to remind him of his family. A successful life would be one that avoided touching the brutal pain of his losses as much as possible.

Having lived through five years of starvation, extreme loneliness and traumatization, he wanted to make food, love and safety last for a lifetime. He wanted to be held and hear his name, remind himself of what he once could do. Tilly no doubt had a heart full of compassion for Alex. She held him at midnight when his dreams were the worst. She admired his strength, his bright spirit and ambition to establish the best deli, selling the best products, just as she wanted to leave the memories of starvation and deprivation behind. The more pedantic German boys paled in comparison to Alex. So successful were they together that in in just two years they were able to move to a much larger store with an apartment above it, which is where I was born in 1954.

My mom Tilly and dad Alex in the early years after the war.

Alex during the early post war years when he was establishing himself in the black market. It's still one of the earliest photos of him, as all photos of childhood and his family were lost.

PART TWO

Chapter 8

A bear in the beer tent

Elke, Straubing, 1958–1963

THE YELLOW VOLKSWAGEN BEETLE SPARKLED IN THE sunlight. Slowly, it made its way along Schlesische Street, heading out of the city. A father with a hat and horn-rimmed glasses sat in the driver's seat. Beside him, with teased brown hair and pearl studs in her ears, his wife looked straight ahead. Behind them, their boy looked down at something in his hands. Maybe he had a *Mickey Mouse* magazine. I wonder where they're going, I asked myself, pressing my face against the inside of the shop window. I wasn't supposed to do that, as my mother had to clean the windowpane pretty well every day. But what could I have done? I was bored, and I imagined that the family in the yellow Bug was driving to the Bavarian mountains. There, they would go for a walk and drink lemonade in a café afterwards. I would have loved to do this with my parents. But this wasn't possible, as my parents had to work in their store all day long.

The small bell above the door jingled again, and a young lady in a knee-length floral dress came in. Every time the door opened, the warm air from outside pushed into the store. The young lady wiped the sweat off her forehead with a pocket handkerchief and ordered three hundred grams of salami, one *mettwurst* and a couple of wieners. My mother, standing behind the counter in her white apron, cut and weighed the sausages and wrapped them in wax paper.

Hopefully, I thought to myself, the woman would leave right away. But no such luck. She started chattering. "My raspberries really like this hot weather—hasn't the weather been just wonderful?"

My mother smiled. For the next few minutes, they discussed the heat and the fierce thunderstorm that had come over Straubing a couple of days ago. My mom joked about how pleasant it was in the cold storage.

I felt like stomping my foot on the ground. Instead, I looked at my stuffed bear, with his black button eyes and a snub nose. The corners of his mouth were turned down and he almost looked a bit sad. That is how I felt too—and I was angry. Today was my fourth birthday and nobody had time for me. I patted my bear on top of his head where the fluffy fur was already worn off a little.

Now the lady was showing my mother her dress. She lifted it by the hem with her fingertips and pulled outwards. "It really does drape well," I heard my mother say. The young lady laughed, turning herself left and then right, the petticoat under her dress rustling.

I held my bear tight, hoping that my mother would see me standing alone at the window, ask the lady to leave, and come over to play with me instead. But that didn't seem to help. I tried holding my head down and looked up sideways at the two of them.

"It was even on sale," the young lady said with a giggle. Then the bell rang again and the next customer, an older man, shuffled through the door.

"*Grüss Gott*, good day, Frau Michalowicz," he said.

"No, not another one," I thought to myself and tried hard to look at the floor even more petulantly than before. Then I noticed that the man was dragging his left foot behind him. I lifted my head and looked at him. He had salt and pepper hair, sideburns, thick glasses and a wrinkled face. But he smiled at me kindly and bent over to pinch me on the cheek.

"What a nice bear you have," he said. Then he turned around and let my mother serve him at the counter.

This man reminded me of my grandfather, Opa Johann, my mother's father, who continued to nurture and care for me after my kind and beloved Oma Maria passed suddenly the year before.

As a therapist now reflecting upon this time, I consider myself lucky that while my parents were in the store working all day, my maternal grandmother Maria took care of me during those defining first three years when we form attachments. My Oma Maria would do anything for her family, or so I have been told by my mother and my uncles Hans and Erwin. But I do not remember her cradling me in her arms. I desperately try to recall how it must have felt to feel her softness around me, but I am drawing a blank. It's like she has never been. But for days after she vanished from my life, I must have expected to see her kind face and her reaching out to hold me close. Maybe I lay in my bed and cried waiting for her to soothe me. I was just a little girl who didn't understand that she herself may have struggled to care for me. And I did not understand what it meant that she was no longer there.

But the person who was there to care for me during the day was my grandfather. He was the one who took over, and it is him I remember. My grandfather's embrace and the intensity of how much we mattered to each other lodged vividly and deeply in my consciousness. When Oma's heart stopped, Opa must have missed her terribly. Having his little granddaughter depend on him must have helped him to deal with the loss of his wife and stay focused. He let himself daydream with me and enjoyed what was left of his life with this little new life beside him. We liked to laugh and didn't take a moment for granted.

Yet his own health was precarious and one year later his body gave out. I was told that on his deathbed he started to yodel. His children who were with him found this startling. "Just before his lungs gave out, he yodeled!" Maybe it was his way of greeting Maria. "He sure sounded happy when he let out the yodel."

A photograph of Maria and Johann hung in my parent's living room. I liked seeing them there—it made me feel they were somehow still with me. But there are no such photos of my paternal grandparents. Not even one of my father's childhood memories could be concretely seen. It was as if it hadn't existed.

But the sadness must have been palpable. I would have liked my mom to talk about Oma and Opa, but she just couldn't. How do you even explain death to a four-year-old, especially if it's the people she has been most attached to? Instead, they told themselves, "Keep moving, don't stop."

Even though they were torn up inside, what mattered now was to be strong for their little one and keep a roof over our heads.

My job as a therapist has been to understand and help people see what feelings they may be hiding from. Most people build fortresses around their vulnerable feelings of sadness, loneliness and shame. This is so they aren't overwhelmed by these feelings. And so it was, with my parents and myself.

I loved sitting on my Opa's lap when he read me stories out of the *Struwwelpeter* book. Every child had one of those scary children's story books. By itself, the picture of Struwwelpeter, the unruly boy on the front cover with his wild hair, red outfit and horribly long fingernails, was frightening. But, with my grandfather by my side, I was curious to open it and look at the other pictures—the bad Friedrich, the Soup Kasper and the Fidgety Philipp. I knew exactly the page where I would find the story of the matches gone wrong. I would have preferred to keep turning the pages, as it made me shudder to see how Pauline went up in flames and the cats Minz and Maunz lifted up their paws and cried bitter tears over her.

Opa would always find simple life lessons in the stories for me to think about, like: "That is why, Elke, you must never play with matches." And I was assured there was something I could do to not go up in flames.

After lunch, when I was supposed to have a short nap, my grandfather always put woolen socks on my feet and covered me with a warm blanket in fall and winter to make sure I wouldn't be cold. Then he read *Struwwelliese* to me. I liked to hear the story about the messy girl over and over and found it funny how she suddenly started dressing herself in fresh clothes and cleaning her room. When the mother praised her daughter at the end of the book and ran her hands over the girl's freshly washed and neatly combed hair, I always imagined it was me. This was another thing I could do: make my parents proud and not cause them any trouble. With that thought, I fell asleep, and when I had woken from my nap he gently combed my blond locks. I also wanted to comb someone, so Opa sat patiently while I ran my hairbrush through his hair.

My favorite thing of all was to walk along the Danube with my grandfather. He held my hand very tight so I could bend over the river's edge and peer into the water. He lifted me up onto the railing of the big castle bridge and wrapped his arms around me tightly so that I could dangle my legs over the railing. The Danube flowed below, wide and dangerous, but I was safe—Opa was there to hold me. When we had enough of looking, he'd lift me off and we'd stroll past the Duke's Castle. Grandpa whistled to himself, sounding just like the birds flying past us. Sometimes we were certain that the finches, chickadees and blackbirds were whistling and chirping back. Then we went up to the city, where we would buy a big crispy pretzel with salt.

I had been with my grandparents every day during the work week for the first three years of my life. Every evening, after his long day at work, my father would pick me up at their home, and we'd drive back to my parents' apartment above the store. Early the next morning, my father brought me back to my grandparents. After my grandmother died, my mother invited my grandfather for lunch on Sundays, the only day the store was closed. It was important to her that he wasn't alone on that day. I stood at the bus stop jumping with excitement until his bus finally rolled down the street. When the door opened with a loud squeak, I ran to him and he picked me up, gave me a kiss on the cheek and stroked my hair.

But at four years old I was standing alone in the store, holding the bear my grandfather had so often carried for me. I looked out through the store window onto Schlesische Street. A long, silver bus drove by, the same bus my grandfather rode to visit us each Sunday. I'd waited for him at the bus stop a few meters from the store, but last Sunday was the first time I didn't wait for him. My mother had woken me that morning, sitting down on my bed. She took my hand and held it.

"Elke," she said, "Elke, Opa is not coming today."

"What, why is that?" I had asked, rubbing the sleep from my eyes.

"Grandfather won't be able to come anymore. He is gone." Tears rolled down her face. "He was too young to die, but he is gone. We just have to be strong, like him, and keep him in our hearts," she said, hugging me to her. I let myself melt against her body and assured her we would be strong and I could feel him in my heart.

As a four-year-old I looked at my mom in awe. She was beautiful, and I loved her soft voice reading to me at night and her soothing words. I could never get enough of her. Her hugging me during her tears meant a great deal; that much I knew. She usually had a tight rein on her emotions. There was usually no time during the day to let tears flow, as there was constantly something to be done. But in the evening, when she tucked me into bed, she could allow herself to soften.

Most people are considered lucky to know their grandfathers. I did not know my dad's father, Arye, but I had known Johann for almost four years. In those years I had formed the closest attachment I had ever felt for a human being. While my parents were attending to the store, the love between Opa and me was pure and something I could count on every day.

At that age, I had only a vague feeling that the effects of the war were lingering, that it had caused my Grandpa Johann much suffering and that he had died far too young as a result. I knew that war was much more menacing and real than *Struwwelpeter* could ever be. War was the cause of all this and nobody had any control over it. I was afraid war could happen again.

At four years old these were my deepest fears.

The old man was just leaving the store with his basket full of sausages when our neighbor wandered in. It is just not going to happen today, I thought to myself, trudging through the store into the back room. There I crouched on the couch and danced my bear back and forth. I pressed my face into his fluffy fur, staring at the door that led to the store. Maybe no more customers will come today, I thought, and my mother will read me a story. That is something she had promised, at least—and it was my birthday.

For a few days, we had been reading "Hansel and Gretel." I wanted to hear it over and over, especially the beginning, when the father had to leave Hansel and Gretel in the forest. I felt sorry for the children, and it brought me to tears when Hansel sprinkled breadcrumbs to mark their path and all the birds of the forest ate them so Hansel and Gretel couldn't find their way back home. My mother had closed the fairy tale book, hugged me tight and explained to me that it wasn't a true story. Just like grandfather had said that Pauline wasn't real. But now my Opa was dead, and that was real.

"What if there is war? Then we would also have to leave home, right?" I kept asking my mother every time we read the story.

"No, we are not at war right now," she said, smiling.

"But grandfather died because he was wounded in the war."

"Elke, the war happened more than twelve years ago. His wounds just didn't heal. There won't be any more war now." Then she took a deep breath, probably because she had had to tell me this many times before.

"If a war comes, I will drop pebbles and find my way back here," I said, trying to find something I could do to make myself feel reassured.

My mother nodded patiently. I turned over in bed and she turned the lights out. "Sleep well," she said, before shutting the door.

In the dark, I folded my hands and began to pray. "Please, God, please make sure that the war doesn't come here ... please ... please, make sure."

I was thinking about all that while I waited in the backroom for my mom. I wanted to continue the story, but I couldn't read yet. So the book lay on the couch next to me and I stared at the door that led to our store. I tried to will that door open and my mom to come in.

The other door, to the left of the kitchen sink, could have stayed shut forever. It led to the courtyard of the production building where the butchers cured meat and made sausages and where the cold storage housed all the huge slabs of beef and pork.

Sure enough, as if I had known this would happen, one of the butchers suddenly swung that door open. He stood in the doorframe wearing a yellow rubber apron with blood running down the front, his black boots shiny with red. He started to yell something at me that sounded like barking. I couldn't understand what he wanted from me and couldn't answer him. I just hugged my bear even tighter against me. Each time I had to breathe in, I held my bear close to my nose, but the smell of raw flesh still reached me. The man called out something about "take the liver." I didn't make a peep, and just tried to breathe as shallowly as possible. Finally, the man was lost for words. He just shook his head, put a tray of dark wobbly looking meat by the sink and slammed the door behind him. Now I cowered on the couch and felt sick and anxious with confusion and the sight and smell of the raw meat. Should I have answered him? Was it important? Had I let my parents down? Would Opa have been disappointed in me?

After what seemed like an eternity, my mother came in and asked me what was happening. She sat down beside me, took me in her arms and said, "Don't be sad. How could you have known what he wanted you to do with the liver? You have only been in the store with us for three days."

After my grandfather died, I felt desperately lonely. I spent my time in the room behind the store, drawing in my coloring books. Every flower, every car, every face. I colored everything on each page then checked how many uncolored pages were still in the book, because I soon realized I would be spending many hours in this room. When my mother had a short break, she rushed through the door and looked at my drawings. But soon the front doorbell would ring, and she had to go back out. Then she would say, "Elke, don't look like that. I have no choice, this is my work," and she would disappear into the store for another hour.

If I was lucky, my father would come by. He would pick me up and turn around with me in circles. I knew that he didn't have much time, but he used every free minute to see me.

Once, a girl in my neighborhood came into the store and asked my mother if I was allowed to go out to play. Since my mother knew her, she gave me permission. I could hardly wait to go to the playground with her. Then it happened. I fell off the teeter-totter and got a huge lump on my forehead. If I could have, I would have hidden it. But while we ate our supper, my parents noticed. They were angry with me and wanted to know how this had happened. Had someone pushed me? Was I not paying attention?

I didn't understand until years later how very protective they were of me. At the time, I thought I was causing them unnecessary trouble and I felt guilty. Even as a little person I felt responsible to help them out, since they were far too busy for problems with me. So, I did my best by spending more time in the room alone, squeezing my teddy bear even harder.

One opportunity for being a regular child was when I could spend time with my Uncle Hans, my mother's brother. About once or twice a week, when his wife was not working, Mom took me in so I could play with my cousin, Hansi, a rambunctious boy a year older than me. I enjoyed being with them, and when I played catch with Hansi in the fields by the Danube, I almost felt like I did when I'd spent time with my grandfather. I wondered—if my father's side of the family had lived—what those uncles and aunts be like. Nobody could tell me exactly why they had all died, but I knew it was because of the war. Yet I considered myself lucky to at least have my Uncle Hans and his family close.

My dad worked hard all week, but once a week on Saturday nights he let loose. For this he took me with him to a friend's restaurant, which also had music and dancing. We ate schnitzel with French fries while he talked to his friends, and Dad laughed and tapped his foot in time to the music. The restaurant was called Mariandl. It was full of diners and the smoke from their cigarettes and cigars. Beer steins clanged as people toasted each other and called out "Prost!" I was the only small child there, but that did not matter to me at all. I was used to being the only child around adults.

The most wonderful part of those Saturday evenings was when the band came on stage. Then I sat right up front, in the first row, looking up adoringly at the musicians and hoping they would play my favorite song, "Charlie Brown." Since I'd first heard the song on the radio, I kept trying to sing it. Even though I didn't understand what this song by The Coasters was about or who Charlie Brown was, I loved to jump back and forth to the beat of the drum.

One night I sat in front of the stage as usual, staring up at the musicians, while my father played cards with his friends. I clasped my hands and hoped that I would soon hear the first bars of my favorite song. But they sang another song that I didn't know. I tugged at the ruffles of my dress, my little feet dangling from the chair. Suddenly, the bass player leaned down, winked at me and picked me up, placing me on the stage beside him. He whispered in my ear, asking what I would like, and I mumbled "Charlie Brown."

Then they let loose. They were playing my favorite song! I moved my feet forwards and backwards to the beat. When the saxophone joined in, I moved my arms to the sound. From up there, I could see my father sitting in the audience, enjoying a pull on his cigarette and somehow looking just like the Marlboro man from the commercial. He was proud of me, I could tell. It felt good to see him smile. I clapped my hands and felt my body vibrating with the loud music. Without thinking about it, I turned in a circle and noticed that my shiny little shoes had stopped in exactly the right spot in the song: the part where it slowed down when they sang about why everybody was always picking on him.

People grinned up at me, calling out "Bravo!" and encouraging me with applause and laughter. From that moment on, I just wanted to listen to music and dance.

A few years later I could finally understand the lyrics of my former favorite song. It was about a boy named Charlie Brown who kept doing silly things at school, provoking the teacher and getting into trouble. The song somehow matched what would happen to me in school a few years later.

Those Saturday evenings were the highlight of the week for Dad and me, and we both loved the commotion and excitement in that place. My mother seldom came out with us. She was exhausted after a long workday at the store and wanted to stay home. She needed privacy to recuperate. My father and I enjoyed it all, until one day at the Volksfest.

Every year, after my birthday in June, I looked forward to the big folk festival in Straubing. The brass band in the big beer tents, riding the ponies, the big carousels and other exciting rides, the raffles, eating crispy chicken and sweet burnt almonds. Even my mother would come along sometimes, but my dad and I usually headed out together to tour the fairgrounds. I dragged my father by the hand all over the grounds, past the people, the freaky cries from the ghost train, the shouts of "Prost!" from the beer tents, and all the way to the boat swing. Nobody could swing as high as we could and the man who worked there knew who we were and tied the belt around our middle without saying a word. First, we would swing back and forth slowly, and I could watch the people walking by and the balloons the children held. I admired the rose-colored, ornate back wall of the ride. Hundreds of small lamps twinkled as we swung higher and higher. My father and I held onto the bars and pushed back and forth to achieve a greater momentum. One time we even succeeded in doing a handstand and hung upside-down while the boat was in the air. I screamed with excitement and my father whooped with glee. When the staff member came over to stop the boat and take off our seatbelts, he said, "You are pretty daring, young lady!" I jumped out of the ship and reached for my father's hand. I could not understand what the man was getting at—my father and I would never have fallen out of the swing. I knew that I could trust my father completely.

After the swing, we went into a beer tent to eat crispy barbequed chicken and drink lemonade for me and beer for Dad. First, we had to find an available seat on one of the benches. We walked through the tent, past singing people who kept raising their huge beer mugs in the air while the brass band on the stage played a typical Bavarian tune. The servers, fully laden with beer mugs and giant trays with plates of dumplings, spaetzle and roast pork, battled their way past us. Every so often we stopped as my father recognized someone and went to chat. He would bend over the table and shout, as it was so loud. I smiled at the people at the table that I recognized from the store, and then I looked around. Every time the servers clomped through the rows with their beer mugs, the floor shook. The ceiling was hung with bundles of wheat. The brass band played a fanfare again and loud shouts of "Prost!" rang out, mugs bumping so powerfully that the beer foam flew out.

Suddenly, I saw a bear coming into the tent through a side entrance. He was big, like the tallest men in the tent, and he walked upright on his hind legs. He had gigantic dark eyes and white fur. When he opened his mouth, I could see his long teeth. I couldn't believe it—what was a bear doing in a beer tent? I squeezed my father's hand. He didn't react because he was talking with a lady sitting at the table. I pulled at his hand and squeezed closer to him.

Then he turned to me. "Elke, what exactly is the matter?" he snapped.

I pointed my finger at the bear that was now coming closer to us. I began to cry and scream, "I want out, I want to get out of the tent, there is a bear!" My heart was leaping out of my chest, I was burning hot, and I could barely see because of my tears.

Leisurely, my father turned in the direction I was pointing. He looked at the bear and looked at me in disbelief. Why aren't the people running away? I thought to myself. Suddenly my father laughed, then lifted me up and walked straight through the rows of benches towards the bear. I squirmed, screeched and flailed my arms. What is he doing? We have to leave the tent! The more I roared and flailed, the more my father grinned and walked even faster in the direction of the animal. I noticed that the people in the tent where staring at us, but I couldn't help myself—I had to scream.

"Come on, Elke," he said, "The bear isn't real. You don't need to be scared." But I didn't believe him. I kicked my feet and hammered my father's shoulders with my fists. When we got to the bear, I turned away and pressed my face against my father's throat. I could hardly believe we were walking toward the bear and not running away as fast as possible. Why would my father do that? The bear would bite us and scratch our faces with his claws, just like I saw in one of the storybooks my grandfather had read to me.

A few moments later, when the bear began talking to me, it slowly dawned on me that it wasn't a genuine bear. My father still held me in his arms and we even took a photo. My eyes were swollen and even my throat felt like it was raw with tears. I still felt the bear was stupid, and I was angry and disappointed with my father.

The bear was obviously a fake and my dad was trying to show me that, but I could not get it. As a professional therapist, I know now how this happens. I still remember the anguish of the little girl thinking over and over, "What if this bear is real after all?" Doubts about what was real suddenly flooded over that little girl like a tidal wave. The war was real, so maybe it would come again? My grandpa wasn't with me and that sure was real. He would know how to make everything better, but he wasn't there. Instead, I was with my father and he sure didn't make me feel safe.

Was it already written in me that I would become a professional who helps people deal with panic attacks? My panic over the bear triggered my dad. He needed to squash this out-of-control feeling of terror and he grabbed me quickly to walk towards the bear. Had he not panicked himself, and reassured me that the bear wasn't real, we could have slowly approached the bear. He ended up forcing me to approach the bear while I was terrified. I had no choice but to squash my out-of-control terror too. But my mistrust lingered. What if the bear was real after all? I was still flooded with emotions of turmoil. Instead of feeling safe I felt angry at my dad for making me feel embarrassed and misunderstood.

Barely a year after the brush with the bear, and much time on my own in the room beside the store, I had my fifth birthday. I could not wait—I would finally be able to attend school. But I was soon disappointed, because I learned I would have to wait until I was six. What game could I invent until then? I came out of my room and walked back and forth in front of the store with my grandfather's brown leather briefcase, pretending I was a student already. Some customers would stop, surprised, and ask, "But Elke, are you old enough to go to school already?"

Then I would answer with a wide grin, "Not yet, but soon."

The night before my first day at the St. Peter Elementary School, I could barely sleep because of my excitement. Finally, finally I would be a schoolchild. The next morning, I put on my best clothes and put my school knapsack over my shoulders. In one hand, I held my school "horn of plenty" that my mother had stuffed with cotton and paper at the bottom and with candies and chocolates at the top. With my other hand, I held her hand as she accompanied me on my first day of school.

I felt comfortable in the classroom. I enjoyed the table that I sat at and thought my teacher was very nice. But I noticed my mother watching some of the other children with a skeptical look. Some of them were not well behaved and kept calling out, hitting one another and interrupting the teachers.

Just before my first summer holiday, I was brooding over homework in the room at the back of the store, when my mother and father sat down with me at the table. First, I asked myself if I had done anything wrong because it wasn't often that they were both able to sit with me at the same time. Maybe it had something to do with getting a report card soon, as Grade One was almost over. But it was something else entirely that they wanted to get off their chests.

"Elke, we have decided to send you to a different school."

"What?" I asked and dropped my pencil. I thought, Is that even possible?

"Elke, wouldn't you rather attend a school where there are only girls?" my father asked, looking at me.

I didn't know how to answer him. Sometimes I was a little scared of the boys and when one of the boys was rude to the teacher, I was embarrassed for him. But the noise and the commotion didn't really bother me. I was just so happy to attend school.

My parents had decided to send me to the Agnes-Bernauer-School, a convent in the middle of Straubing. "I will drive you there every day, since it is too far for you to walk," my father explained. "It is worth it to me, because I want you to be able to learn in a calm environment."

I nodded, as I could tell that this meant something to him, and it was clear that my parents had been discussing this for a while already.

"You know, school was very important to me when I was your age. I learned so much there. If the war had not happened, I would have gone to school much longer," he said. "You should be able to have this opportunity. Your mother will pick you up every day after school."

"I find boys stupid, anyways," I mumbled, and kept scribbling in my notebook.

In retrospect, I think my father was alarmed by the sight of raucous boys around me. He was simply too traumatized by the men in the camps. His worry made him want to put me in the safest environment possible and out of the way of cruel boys.

Before I knew it, I, the daughter of a Jew, was attending a Catholic convent. On the first day my mother brought me to school in our car, an Opel, in my favorite color of metallic aqua blue. She parked the car and went with me up the steps to the formidable wooden door of the convent school. I stood with my school backpack in front of this gigantic building, biting my lip. My stomach hurt. What if the other girls didn't like me? What if I couldn't find a friend?

Mom pushed the door open and a nun with a long, flowing, dark cloak came toward me. The nun introduced herself as Sister Michaela and my mom smiled warmly, saying our names. Before rushing back to the store, Mom whispered to me and gave my arm an encouraging squeeze. "Be a good girl, but have the courage to say something, if someone asks you."

Sister Michaela took me to the bench in the second row of my appointed classroom. I sat and took out my chalkboard, feeling prepared for anything that might happen. In the first hours of lessons, I watched the Sister closely. I was fascinated with the many layers of cloth she wore, and that not a single hair was visible from under her veil.

After recess, where everything was a lot quieter and nobody roughhoused or screamed, the Sister stood next to me and presented a girl with a short, brown page cut. "This is Ursula," the nun said. "She will be your bench mate." Ursula sat down on the bench right next to me, pulled out her small chalkboard and looked at mine, just as I was checking hers. Our gazes met, and we grinned at each other. From that moment, I liked this girl with the warm brown eyes.

After school, I noticed that Ursula and I had almost exactly the same route home and felt certain that the Sister knew this and seated us next to each other for that reason.

I soaked up Sister's every word during our lessons. With great purpose she walked through the rows, her habit flowing behind her importantly. When she scolded us, her seriousness made a deep impression. But she was always fair, treated everyone the same, and when one of the girls was injured, she held her in her arms and comforted her. She often laughed and gave us the feeling that she cared about us.

At the end of the Second Grade, Sister Michaela held the first big exam. We prepared for this for weeks and I was happy to sit in the room behind the store and practice. My mother even had to interrupt me occasionally. "Elke, now it is time for a break." But I couldn't be bothered. I liked to learn.

When the big day came, some of the other girls told me how much they were afraid of the exam. One of them was shaking, her face white as chalk. I was calm and looked forward to the test. During the exam, I noticed there were a few questions that could easily trick you if you weren't paying exact attention. I had to smile, as I had the feeling that I had seen through this. I wasn't going to fall for it, and I even included a comment about that in my answers.

A week later, Sister Michaela stood in front of us with a stack of papers. She had corrected all of the exams. Calmly, she handed them out. To one girl, she said, "Well done" and to another, "You should pay closer attention to the questions." The classroom was so quiet you could hear a pin drop. When she stood at my table, she lifted her head and looked at me. "Elke," she said seriously, "I would like to talk to your parents about the exam. Can you let them know?"

With tears in my eyes, I swallowed and nodded. What exactly had I done wrong? Then she put my exam on the table. I hadn't made a single mistake. But what wasn't right? During recess, the other girls discussed their results, but what could I say? Something was wrong. On the school grounds, I made the decision not to say anything to my parents for now. But two hours later, after school, I came to the conclusion that this wouldn't help and I would get into even more trouble. And trouble was the last thing I wanted—for my parents and me.

My mother picked me up from school and I tore open the car door and started chattering—I hadn't made any mistakes, I didn't know what was wrong, nothing was marked in red—but the teacher wanted to speak with her or my father.

Mom wasn't exactly sure what was happening. "Elke, slow down, what is the matter?" I explained it again and again, then I tried not to mention the exam anymore.

My mother was not the type to put things off, so first thing in the morning, she came in to see the Sister. We found her in the auditorium.

"Frau Michalowicz, how nice to see you," Sister Michaela said, as friendly as usual. The sentence echoed through the high-ceilinged room. I was allowed to stay and be a part of the conversation. So I stood next to my mother and stared at the nun.

"This has to do with the exam that we recently held in class," Sister said.

"Yes, Elke told me about it." my mother replied.

"Elke's results are completely different from those of the other girls."

"Different? What do you mean?" my mother asked nervously. I flinched. Had Sister not corrected anything because everything was wrong? This was something I hadn't even thought about. I took a deep breath.

"For goodness sake, there is no reason to worry," said Sister with a brief laugh. "This is good news. I mean, different in a positive sense. I have never experienced this with an eight-year-old. It is really remarkable that Elke can think so far ahead and that she couldn't be duped by even one of the questions."

Now my mother had to smile. "Oh," she said with a loud sigh of relief. "Then everything is okay. Should I be doing something different?"

"I would recommend that she be signed up to postsecondary education gymnasium after she finishes primary school." In the German education system, *Gymnasium* has nothing to do with physical education but is the highest level of secondary education possible. It leads to university. That much I knew already.

I was so excited—I would be able to go to school longer! I imagined all of the things I would experience. I would have liked to hug the Sister, because I was so grateful to her. In that moment, I made the decision to also become a convent nun.

Only a few months later, I was with the Sisters not just in the morning, but also in the evening. Mom had been taken to the hospital in Mallersdorf. Shortly before being brought there, she told my father and me that she had been feeling severe stomach pains for days already.

We now spent every evening there. After I had finished telling my mother about school, my father allowed me to visit the small chapel in the hospital. Every evening there was a little mass with lots of hymns and I rushed through the long hallways to get there in time. The hallway walls were painted pea green, and here and there a door would open, a nun emerging from a patient's room. It smelled like the liquid that people rubbed on their hands to make them clean. When I walked past a dispenser, I tried to hold my breath so I wouldn't have to breathe it in.

On the way to the chapel, I walked by a painting of Jesus Christ. It was gigantic and surrounded by a majestic golden frame. I looked into the eyes of the painted Jesus and inside myself said, "Hello." How much I envied the nuns who walked by with their heads bowed. They seemed so satisfied, so serene. Very different from the people on the street who raced by and looked grumpy. The Sisters had found their path. They knew exactly what they could expect and that Jesus would always be there for them. I thought about how nice it would be to have this kind of certainty in my life.

There was another reason I wanted to be a Catholic convent nun. Often, I eavesdropped on my father, when he spoke to his customers in an unusually quiet voice. There weren't many people he talked to like that—just the people who came to the store almost daily. One time he had whispered to a lady over the counter, "Frau Schulz, you know, our kind always lives in fear."

Frau Schulz had looked at him with concern, the corners of her mouth pulled down. "Oh, Herr Michalowicz, you shouldn't have any more worries these days."

"But, yes. As a Jew, one never loses it …" he had answered her in a quiet voice.

"No, really, that was such a long time ago," she had answered, shaking her head.

Jew? What did that mean? I knew that my father wasn't Catholic, like most of the Straubingers, like my mother and myself. My father explained to me that he only believed in the Old Testament and not in the New Testament, like we studied in school. He had also explained once that bad things had happened to the Jews in the war, and to his family, and that was why I didn't know any of them.

Why did my dad whisper when he talked about being a Jew? Why did he seem so full of sorrow and Frau Schulz so consoling in looking for the right words? So, I thought to myself, how could I make this better? For sure, if I became a nun, then no one would ever guess that my father was a Jew. I could protect him. That would make everyone feel better, including myself.

Now I sat on one of the benches in the hospital chapel every night. A young nun waited for me there. She put her hand deep within the folds of her skirt pocket and pulled out a little picture lithograph. She took my hand and put the delicate, orange-colored paper on it. By now I had learned how the picture worked, how it moved on its own accord when you blew on it. It was the best picture of all and I wanted to blow on it immediately. But I knew how to control myself and tried to be calm and not so fidgety, just like the young nun.

The nun asked, "How is your mother doing?"

I told her what my father had said: that my mother was absolutely certain that she would soon recover. The young nun smiled and stroked my hair. I would have enjoyed having her as my teacher. But by then I had already moved on to Third Grade and now had a new nun teacher who scared me, Sister X. She was as mean as could be, and not fair, like Sister Michaela.

The door to the chapel opened and other people came in. I said goodbye to the young nun and the first thing I did at the door was to breathe on the picture. It rolled in from all sides and for a brief time it looked like the Madonna on the picture was alive. I saved every one of those small lithographs the nuns gave me in a special little box at home.

While I was running through the hospital back to my mother's room, I thought about what I could expect the next day. Since Sister X, I dreaded going to school. I still loved to study, diligently did my homework and tried to be as good as possible. But she did not seem to notice. She was always mean to me. It didn't matter what the other children in the class did, she stood menacingly over my desk in front of me, yelled and often hit me.

I didn't say anything at home, of course, as I didn't want to worry my father, who had to run everything on his own now, with my mother in the hospital. Our store had expanded to the point that we now had several employees working there. But he was the one who woke me up, combed my hair, made my breakfast and drove me to school.

In the classroom, every time I was so unfairly and harshly treated, I wondered what was behind it. I had often wished my parents were a bit more like the parents of the other children. That my father was Catholic; that he spoke Bavarian like the others, not with a strange accent. Maybe that was the reason Sister X didn't like me. Things at home were not normal and my mother had been in the hospital for weeks. My thoughts centered on this nun, but I always came to the same conclusion, that everything would change once I became a convent nun myself. Then she would accept me for sure.

Of course, everything happened differently.

My father picked up my friend Ursula and me from school just like every afternoon. As if she had practiced, it just exploded out of her: "Herr Michalowicz, I have to tell you this now—Sister X is so mean to Elke!" She had tears in her eyes and her voice shook. My father looked in the rearview mirror and asked, "What do you mean, Ursula?" She proceeded to tell him all the things that the nun had said and done to me. My father concentrated on the road but kept asking questions and looking at both of us through the rearview mirror. I stared out of the window and bit my lip. How could she say those things? Why was she doing this?

I figured out later that maybe I should be grateful to Ursula—the secret was out now. But at the time I was devastated. I could not pretend to myself anymore that the nun was mistreating me and worse yet, now my father would have to get involved.

The next day, my father came to the school and spoke to Sister X. They stood in a private room and I sat at a bench off to the side, opening and closing the zipper of my little wallet at least a hundred times. She started off sugar-sweet and tried to convince my dad that she was a kind teacher. He wasn't buying it and kept questioning her. I could not help but get upset when Sister X tried to dupe my dad by asking if he wanted to talk to the other children and ask them if she treated me fairly. What a con artist she is, I thought. I hope Dad doesn't fall for this. And he didn't—he was getting enraged that she thought she would get away with that move.

Now that he had flushed her out as an insincere and disrespectful human being, he would not stand for it. He told her in no uncertain words that of course the other children would stand up for her; they would be afraid they she would turn her wrath on them! Now he could not be stopped. I tried hard not to listen to him accusing her of hating to see a man like him live and bring a child like me into her flock. He told her if she truly felt like that, she should take her aggressions out on a piece of wood and not on innocent children. She would never touch a hair on his daughter's head again. **She** should practice what she was preaching and **be** a nun, not the handmaiden of the SS. I wasn't sure what he meant by that, but Sister X seemed to be visibly sweating under her habit and squirming uncomfortably. I hoped my father would be able to calm down again.

I tried not to think what would happen as soon as my father walked out the door. "Zip," my purse said, again and again. How would I ever live this down? My father walked over to me and took a deep breath. He knelt in front of me and took my hands. "Elke, we have settled this. You don't have to be scared anymore. You can go back to the classroom now."

He turned away again, giving Sister X a scorching look before disappearing through the door. That was my father's fierce survivor spirit erupting like a volcano. He would not let the injustice that had been done to him be done to his daughter. He had risen from the dead and he had brought a daughter into this world. Anybody messing with his daughter better watch out.

Sister X was visibly shaken. But she composed herself quickly and her face turned cold and foreboding while she whispered to me. "God can see everything. He knows what you did." She pulled me up from the bench and ushered me back into the room. Well, in that case, he can also see what you did, and I should be quite all right then, I thought to myself as I sat back down in my usual spot.

From then on, Sister X simply ignored me. From my years of experience in the room behind the store, I knew exactly how to stay quiet and make the best of this. No matter how painful Sister X was trying to make things, I resolved to not let her get to me. I held tight to my sadness and anger for the next year and concentrated on schoolwork. And I had something else to look forward to: Mother was finally able to leave the hospital and come home.

Christmas when I was three years old. My dad's number tattoo is visible on his left arm.

This photograph of me at age five was my mom's favorite.

Here I am delighted to finally go to school. Every student gets a school cone filled with sweets on their first day of school.

Chapter 9

The coincidence

Straubing, 1963

I WAS NINE YEARS OLD WHEN A CHANCE ENCOUNTER changed everything.

I came home from school one day and found my father napping on the couch in the small room behind the store. I sat down quietly at the table that functioned as the kitchen and dining table, as well as my desk, and started working on a math problem. Looking at my father, I noticed that his chest was slowly moving up and down, his breathing, quiet and even. With just a little *pffff* breathing out, he seemed to be sleeping so deeply that nothing could wake him up. This made me happy.

My parents hadn't talked to me about it, but I had picked up that he hadn't been able to sleep for weeks. He woke every night, covered in sweat and screaming. There were deep shadows under his eyes, and his skin was pale. His gaze seemed worried and exhausted.

Tired and weak, he dragged himself into the meat production area early in the morning. During the midday break, when the store was closed, he lay on the couch in the room behind the store, but there, his rest was often interrupted. A worker would open the door with a question, or the phone would ring because someone wanted to place an order. When he was finally able to fall asleep, my mother would come in to wake him. Lunch break was over—it was time to unlock the store again.

With my father's sleep being such a rare commodity, I wanted to be as quiet as possible. I ran the pencil over my notebook ever so carefully and when I should have sharpened it, I decided to leave it.

Suddenly, he twitched. The blanket that lay over his feet fell to the ground. He pulled his hands against his body and pulled up his knees.

I put the pencil aside and stared at him. He mumbled something in his sleep that I couldn't quite make out, but I had the impression that he was speaking Yiddish. Suddenly he started flapping his hands and screaming.

I was scared but didn't have the courage to approach him, so I just sat there and put my hands over my ears. The screaming grew louder. Then, with a jerk, he pulled himself upright and opened his eyes. It was deadly quiet in the room. Tears shone in his eyes, and he gasped for air. He hid his face behind his hands.

Only when he slowly moved his fingers up through his hair to slick it back did I dare speak.

"Are you okay?" I asked softly.

He hadn't noticed that there was someone in the room with him, and it startled him. When he saw me, he tried to smile a little. "Yes, yes, everything is okay." My father stood up, came over to stroke my hair, gave me a kiss on the cheek and went back into the store.

That afternoon, I looked for him, but he wasn't in the store, the cold storage or the sausage kitchen. And the delivery truck was in the yard. In his stead, my mother stood behind the counter in the store. When he came home for dinner that night, my father told us that he had been to see the doctor.

"What did he say?" my mother asked.

"That I should go to Munich, to see someone who is familiar with this," my father said. He took a handwritten note from his jacket pocket, showing an address in Munich the doctor had written down.

"How are you going to get there? We can't just close the store, and you won't be able to go alone," my mother said, looking at the address on the paper. "You have never driven there with the car before."

"The doctor said that it wasn't too far away from the main train station."

"You know perfectly well that going by train isn't possible." My mother shook her head.

I sat between them, looking from one to the other. She was right. I knew my father was not able to ride on a train. He had once told me that he had been taken from one concentration camp to another during the war, always by train. So many people were squeezed into the compartments that there was almost no room to stand or sit. They had traveled like this for days, exhausted, hungry and sick. Many died on these trains, and their corpses were moved into the corners of the compartments. After a few hours, they began to stink.

Each day, for days at a time, there was only one stale piece of bread to eat and a sip of water to drink. My father was so hungry that his stomach began to bloat. But for him, the worst thing was that he was without his family, without his friends. When he told me about the trains, the feeling of being alone and abandoned, I could feel that was something really terrible. I asked him how people went to the bathroom on the trains. He had answered that there wasn't a toilet. After this, I didn't ask any more questions, and tried to force my thoughts away from the trains. I was surprised that he told me that much.

"I can't help it," my father said now, swallowing. "If I want to visit this doctor in Munich, I will have to take the train."

"How are you going to do that?" my mother asked.

"I'll go on a weekday, when there isn't a lot going on in the store." He paused briefly. "I will take the train to Munich next week."

I couldn't stand the thought of my father going alone. I put my ham sandwich back on the plate and said loudly, "I'll go with you!"

My parents looked at me. He definitely needed to go and maybe it would help to have me along. Nobody expected this to be an ordinary outing. But I had two goals in mind: I wanted to take my father to the specialist who could help him face whatever these terrible things of his past were, and I really wanted to see Munich.

Several of my friends had already been to the city with their parents. They had told me there were huge stores with a lot of things you couldn't buy at the Straubing market. They had raved about the restaurants, the street musicians and Marienplatz, where my friends had witnessed figurines dancing to orchestral bells in the town hall's tower.

In the evening, as I lay in bed, I imagined how I would spend the day with my father. In my imagination, it was a vacation day—something I hadn't experienced with my parents since they were never able to leave the store.

In the meantime, my father began preparing himself for the train ride. The next morning, he drove to the train station to buy some magazines and look around. It didn't bother him as much as he'd expected, and during the lunch break, he told us that he was convinced he would be able to get on the train. After the weekend, my mother drove us to the train station in the morning.

From the moment he stood on the platform, my father was not himself anymore. He did not say a single word but bit his lips over and over. He nervously tapped his feet and sweat beads ran down his temples. I took my father's sweat-covered hands and pulled him over to the timetables. I tried to calm him by reading out the arrival and departure times of the trains. But then a voice on the loudspeaker announced that the train to Munich would be arriving shortly, so I had to break off my reading.

"Elke, I won't be able to do this today," my father stammered, his face ashen.

He trembled when I took his hand. Then we both stumbled out through the big door of the railway station towards a taxi. We had not succeeded. I was sad because I wanted to help him, and I also wanted to see the big city. My mother was disappointed when she looked out the shop window and saw us climbing out of the taxi. My father didn't speak for a couple of hours afterwards—he simply continued his work at the store.

"You can do this, Alex," my mother encouraged him. "It will work the next time. And when you see the doctor, he will be able to help."

After that first attempt, my father rallied and renewed his efforts. A week later, my mother brought us back to the train station. I was now on summer holidays and had the feeling I wouldn't be spending my holidays at Garda Lake like other children, but instead, at the Straubing train station.

The day began just like that of our failed attempt. Even at breakfast, my father couldn't say a single word. He looked into space, chewing his bun, lost in thought. My mother again packed a bag with provisions: a bun with ham and a pickle for my father and one without a pickle for me, two apples and a bar of chocolate. Then she dropped us off at the train station.

Again, I watched the large clock and hoped we would be sitting on the train to Munich in twenty minutes. My father bought himself a ticket. This was a good sign, I hoped. I summoned my courage and told him that all my girlfriends were going to the outdoor pool this afternoon and I had told them that I couldn't come along because I was going to Munich. He just nodded.

When we were standing on the platform, I leaned forward to look at the train tracks. My father's hands began to tremble, but at least we were still waiting for the train. I prayed that we would stay here and not return home this time. From afar, I heard the whistle of the approaching train, then the speakers crackled to life, announcing the departure to Munich.

I could hardly believe it: my father and I were still on the platform. I heard the rumble of the wheels, the hissing of the brakes. The train rushed past us, moving slower until it finally stood still. I looked at my father in disbelief. He stared straight ahead; his lips pressed firmly together. Just in front of our noses, a door opened and a young woman with a baby carriage, an elderly woman with a walking stick, and two boys stepped out.

I almost asked my father, "What's going on? Why aren't we turning around?"

I felt my heart beat faster. Perhaps we would actually make it this time. With one leap, my father jumped into the train and pulled me after him. He stormed into the compartment and let himself fall into a seat by the window. I sat next to him. After a few seconds, he stood up and opened the top hatch of the window. He remained standing with his eyes closed, breathing loudly.

From the outside, we heard an announcement coming from the loudspeaker, and with a light jerk, the train started moving. In the seats behind us, children laughed and joked, a couple chatted. Then the conductor arrived, asking for tickets. My father cowered on his padded seat, his face chalk-white, while he handed over our ticket. The conductor looked at him strangely but moved on without comment.

"Just breathe in and out," I whispered to my father. "Look out the window at the horizon." This was what my mother had advised me to say in case of an emergency. Somehow, it felt silly—a nine-year-old telling her father what to do. But he listened to my advice. His feet tapped nervously back and forth and sweat ran down his temples. He closed his eyes again.

Seeing him like that, I thought, how much his face has fallen in, how pale and weak he looks.

To distract myself, I opened the lunch bag Mom had prepared and bit into my ham sandwich. For the next two hours, we stayed quiet. He seemed to be coping and I did not want to disrupt this in any way. As we approached the main train station in Munich, the train started to slow. As soon as my father noticed, he was up like a shot. I tried to keep up with him as we hurried through the compartment and jumped off the train with him as soon as the doors opened.

It wasn't until we were sitting in a taxi, driving along wide streets lined with tall houses, that I noticed my father was feeling better. He began to chat with the taxi driver, even laughing. We'd made it. We had arrived in Munich.

Now that my father was back to his usual self, I let go of any thoughts about the journey. I looked out the window to watch women with teased hair and fancy shopping bags. We passed a young woman in high heels who looked like one of the models in the magazine my mother always read. People sat in outdoor cafés drinking coffee and eating pastries and ice cream. They stood in front of the huge shop windows, admiring the clothes and goods.

I would have loved to drive through the streets forever to watch the people in this vibrant city, but we soon arrived at the doctor's office. While my father went to speak to the specialist, I was supposed to stay in the waiting room. There I discovered the biggest rocking horse I had ever seen. I first stroked its velvety fur and ran my fingers through its mane. Then I sat on the saddle and imagined I was Little Joe from *Bonanza*. This was a show I looked forward to every Sunday. The voices in the dubbed German version didn't match the moving lips of the characters, but I loved them anyway. I pretended to ride over the prairie with Joe until my father came out and said, "Come, Elke, we'll get ice cream now."

My father took me to a busy main street called Leopold Street. We admired the cakes and pastries in the cafés and listened to street musicians. I petted a small dog. At every ice cream parlor, we stopped to consider whether the flavors were right for us. We laughed and talked about which was our favorite.

This is what a vacation must feel like, I thought and beamed at my father, who had just bought me a large scoop of chocolate ice cream in a waffle cone. As my lips touched the cold creaminess, I knew that this was the best ice cream I had ever eaten.

We passed many people on the streets. At a flower stand, I stopped and looked at the buckets of roses the woman was selling. Then I spotted a girl who seemed the same age as me—and she was wearing a pink headband. I wiped my mouth with the napkin and turned to my father. "Do you see that girl? Can I have a headband like that, please?"

But my father was no longer by my side. He had stopped a few meters behind me. He wasn't moving and was staring at the pavement. Is he ill? I asked myself. Did I say something wrong? I went to him but before I reached him, he turned away and hurried back in the direction we came from. Perhaps he lost something?

"Jacob, Jacob," my father suddenly shouted. He seemed to be chasing someone. Then a man in the crowd stopped and slowly turned around. I caught up to my father, gasping for air.

"Alex, is that you?" the man asked, looking at my father. "No, no, it can't be."

The man started to cry and fell into my father's arms. They sobbed and hugged each other. Everyone stared at them. People in the surrounding cafés put their drinks down and whispered to each other. Some passersby shook their heads. I just thought, How embarrassing. My father says he doesn't know anyone in Munich. What is all this about?

Even though I was embarrassed by all the people watching, I quickly realized that something extraordinary was happening.

My father and Jacob stood very close and took turns whispering to each other in the language my father sometimes babbled when he was half asleep. I could make out a few words. Suddenly, they both began laughing out loud while tears streamed down their cheeks. I didn't know what was going on but it moved me to see my father like that, and I also started to cry.

"Jacob, this is my daughter, Elke," my father said, pointing at me.

The man bent down and studied me with intense brown eyes. He whispered, "You are a little angel, do you know that? You're alone with your father in Munich? Where is your mother?"

My father sighed, "It's too bad she is not here. She had to stay in Straubing, where we live now."

"Who would have thought such a thing could happen?" said the man, wiping his face with a white handkerchief. My father patted him on the shoulder. "Today," he said slowly, "I am in Munich for the first time in my life. If I hadn't walked down Leopold Street at exactly this time, we would have never bumped into each other. Finally, I know that someone from my past has survived."

He began to sob again and buried his face in his hands.

"My parents, my sisters, my brothers, all dead. You are the only one who survived."

The man grabbed my father by the shoulders. "Alex, Alex! What are you talking about? Don't you know?"

"What do you mean?"

"Your sister, Hanna! She is alive. She lives with her family in Canada."

My father stared with an open mouth, his face going as pale as it was in the train station in Straubing.

"Hanna? That's not possible!"

The man opened his briefcase and handed a piece of paper to my father. "Here," he said. "That's her address in Montreal. And I'll write down mine as well."

On the train ride home, my father told me that Jacob was his childhood friend. He had immigrated to Australia after the Second World War and was only in Munich this afternoon to clear up some paperwork. It was a coincidence that he had Hanna's address in his briefcase.

The train ride went by like a dream. My father didn't even seem to realize he was on a train. He talked about his sister and I peppered him with questions.

"Does this mean we will visit her in Canada? How long does it take to fly there? Do you think we will see her soon?" He answered with a smile. "We'll see her soon, Elke. Soon." When we arrived in Straubing, we saw my mother waiting on the platform. How would she react when we told her what happened?

We jumped off the train and ran to her. My father and I talked at the same time, laughing and crying all at once. My mother stood and stared at us. Then she ushered us to the car, drove us home and brewed a pot of hot herbal tea. For the rest of that day, the store stayed closed.

In the meantime, my father and I had calmed down and were able to tell her what happened in Munich in the right order.

Mom listened quietly, then said, "What you are talking about was not a coincidence. It was destiny. You were in Munich on this exact day for a certain reason, and it was not your doctor's appointment."

"That is true," Dad said. "The doctor couldn't really help me. For that, I didn't have to go all the way to Munich."

"Alex, it doesn't matter," my mother said, reaching for his hand. "This trip brought you more than you ever expected."

Chapter 10

Moving apart to come closer together

Straubing, 1963–1967

FROM THAT DAY ONWARD, EVERYTHING IN MY FAMILY revolved around my father's sister.

While my mother went to the city the next morning to buy airmail envelopes and international stamps, our assistant took over the work in the store. My father sat in the back room at the table and tried to write a letter to his sister. He threw one crumpled paper after another into the garbage can.

I sat on the couch and flipped through the pages of an atlas. With my fingers, I tried to measure how far it was from Straubing to Montreal. Now and then I looked up and watched my father. He began to write, sometimes serious, sometimes cheerful—then suddenly another rustle and another paper ball flew.

When my mother came back from her errand, she said, "Are you finished?"

He shook his head. "I do not know what to write."

It had been more than twenty-three years since he'd seen his sister for the last time in 1940. Each day, for all of those years, he thought of his family. He kept writing to the Red Cross to search for them, but eventually he started believing none of them had survived. From one day to the next, everything had changed—and now he could not find the right words to write to his sister.

My mother sat on the chair next to him, clicked a ballpoint pen and began to write our address on the envelope she had just bought. "Ballpoint pens are good, they don't run like fountain pens when it rains," she told me, "so that Hanna can read our address and write us back." After all those years, my mother did not want to take any chances of our letter getting lost.

Once the letter was mailed, for the next three weeks, my father waited every day for the postman who brought letters to us in the shop. The postman was surprised, because my father had never had time to talk. Suddenly Dad wanted to know everything about the delivery of mail—how long it took to get a letter from another country, or whether he would be notified if the address was wrong. I imagined the various things that could have happened to the letter.

Perhaps it had fallen to the floor in the big post office. Perhaps the postman in Canada could not decipher my mother's handwriting. Perhaps the address Jacob had given us in Munich wasn't correct? My father was probably having similar thoughts. He was more restless than usual. When he sat in a chair, he tapped his feet or drummed his fingers on the table the whole time.

On the last day of my summer holidays, I knew from the look on my father's face that a letter from Hanna for us had arrived: he smiled, his eyes shone. Carefully, like a precious treasure, he carried the light blue envelope through the shop into the adjoining room. My mother did something I had never seen before: she wrote a sign with the words: "Temporarily closed—we open again at 2:00 p.m." and hung it on the glass door.

The envelope had large colorful stamps and postmarks on it and looked very different from ours. We quietly sat around the table. With a letter opener, my mother slowly slit open the envelope and took out the paper inside. Her voice trembled as she read it to us. Hanna had written the letter in Yiddish, which my mother and I could more or less understand because it sounds close to German.

"My dearly beloved Alex, dearest Tilly and dearest Elke ..."

Already after the first words I realized that Hanna was experiencing the same things as my father. She too was overjoyed to have found him again. My father had to blow his nose.

"At first, I did not look closely at your envelope. But after I had opened it, everything around me began to spin. Fortunately, I was in my kitchen and could immediately sit down on a chair. I spent a very long time reading your letter again and again. The first few days after that I ran up and down the house, crying and screaming like a little child. Since I have found out that you are alive, Alex, and that you have a family, all my memories and feelings came back up. I thought my head would burst."

After those lines, my mother had to take a break. My father went out into the yard to get fresh air, and my mother gulped a glass of water. I just wanted her to continue reading.

In the next few paragraphs Hanna told us about her family and the house and described the neighborhood where she lived in Montreal. Almost every sentence included "you will see" or "when you are here." I felt that she really wanted to get to know us.

At the end, she wrote, "Alex, please come to Canada as fast as you can. Bring your family with you! You will understand that I will not travel to Germany. I cannot believe that you actually live in that country, that you are letting your daughter grow up there ..."

I imagined flying to Canada with my parents. Hanna would pick us up with her family and we would decide to live there forever. I would go to a school in Canada and not in Straubing anymore—everything would be much easier and more beautiful. What I found most amazing was that a part of my family spoke English!

When my father drove me to school the next morning, I told him about the plans I had made in the night. "Father, I would like to learn English."

"That's a good idea," he said, giving me a kiss on the cheek. Nevertheless, I had the feeling that he had not been listening to me at all. He was so lost in thought since we had met Jacob.

On the first day back at school, I proudly reported to all my girlfriends that I had an aunt who lived far away on another continent. In the afternoon, I had just come to the store from school when my father drove quickly into the yard. He braked with a jerk. He had been to a travel agency that morning and had inquired about flights to Montreal. He hurried to my mother behind the counter. "Tilly, I really do not know if I will be able to do this," he stammered.

In the travel agency, they told him that the flight from Munich took more than ten hours. It had become clear to him that first he had to go back to Munich by train and then spend a longer period of time trapped in a plane. He was aware that he could not get out of a plane as easily as a train; there were no stops for at least ten hours. It must have sounded like a lifetime to him.

For much of the next year my mother and I were busy trying to convince him to brave it. We came up with different ideas about how he could do it. The advice from the doctor in Munich was less helpful: he said my father should not talk about what he had experienced in his youth and instead take sleeping pills and do relaxation exercises. So, my father listened to cassettes at midday to relax his muscles and shut off. But all this did not alter the fact that he could not sleep, let alone get into an airplane.

For over a year I still hoped that he could overcome his anxieties, but I could tell he had tried everything to persuade himself. He just couldn't. The three suitcases, which my mother had bought a week after Hanna's letter had arrived, lay unused on top of the large wardrobe in the bedroom. We wrote letters to Canada and received mail from Hanna. After a lot of back and forth, it was finally decided that Hanna would come to Straubing with her family.

This presented some other problems. Hanna could still not understand why my father lived in Germany after all that had happened. He was even married to a German woman, a Catholic, and had a daughter with her. What would she think if she knew her brother had a daughter who wanted to be a nun!

One evening, as we drank tea with lemon after closing the shop, my father sat next to me on the couch.

"Elke, what would you think about converting to the Jewish faith?"

Jewish faith? I almost choked on the hot tea and had to cough. How could he even ask me that?

He took the cup from me and placed it on the small table. "If you and your mother converted to Judaism before Hanna visits us with her family, it would make things much easier. What do you think?"

He smiled at me. I felt he was glad that he had finally been able to ask. Maybe it would help him if I could agree? Hanna and the family had promised to come, and with that, becoming a nun was out of the question. I had to consider the new circumstances. Change wasn't bad, it meant excitement. A whole new world was opening up with new possibilities. Whatever the world was, I wasn't sure.

I looked at my mother, who sat at the table stirring her tea. "What do you think, Mama?"

"At least let's be open to the idea," she said, taking a sip. "There are a few other families in Straubing who have done the same thing. A friend of your father's also married a woman who then converted to Judaism. Their children are growing up with the Jewish faith. "

My first thought was school. What would the other girls think when I was suddenly no longer Catholic? Would that be noticeable? Would they exclude me? "Ahh," I groaned. "Suddenly everything will be different. And what about my friends? What will they say?"

My mother got up from the table and sat on the other side of me, her head lying on her hands. She sighed. I had the feeling she was sad. Although she sat next to me, she felt so far away. "We can't change what happened and just have to deal with what is." She raised her head, took me in her arms and said, "If they are really your friends, they will not care. Let's sleep on it for a night. We don't have to decide today. And maybe it's not as bad as you think. There are many new things that are a part of this that you will surely find interesting."

She must have figured I could deal with whatever it was I was facing better than my dad. He may have a nervous breakdown or not be able to cope with his sister's arrival. I, on the other hand, would adapt.

As I lay in my bed that evening, I longed for my grandfather, as I so often did. I imagined how he would listen to me, how he would help me make sense of all the confusion and the strange feelings. I imagined I could snuggle up to him and he would say to me, "Your parents have most likely been thinking about this decision for a while now. And it's not the end of the world."

I would have answered him, "Opa, do you think they might change their minds?"

In his deep, calming voice he would say, "Everything is possible, Elke. But I would not have too much hope." He would take me in his arms and gently rock me until I nodded off. With these thoughts of my grandfather, I fell asleep.

In the next few days, it became more and more clear that I would not be able to influence the changes about to happen. I had no choice but to do what seemed to make my parents the happiest. The only thing I could change was how I handled the situation. My mother had already brought up the most important point in our conversation—new is interesting. This is what I would focus on. So converting to Judaism became a great adventure for me. I found it exciting to learn Hebrew. It felt like a new world was opening up to me. Along with this, I practiced English with a dictionary, because when my aunt visited us with her family, I wanted to be able to introduce myself at least.

Despite all the excitement about change, I had a funny feeling in my stomach. I had to clarify something that kept bothering me: I had a guilty conscience about Jesus. So, I sneaked into the church of the Ursulinen on a school day and sat on one of the wooden benches where I had so often prayed devoutly. I looked around, admiring the gigantic colorful paintings on the walls and the ceiling, the religious figures, the shining gold. I folded my hands and whispered, "Dear God. Please do not be mad at me. It is not so bad if I change to the Jewish faith now. It does not mean anything, because I will always believe in an Almighty God, who I can feel around me and can protect us." I turned around to make sure nobody was listening to me.

"You know," I continued to whisper, "I feel there is something sacred here, when I sit on the bench and look at the cross. But it also happens when I am in the synagogue, and my father sings something. So, it does not really matter what religion we belong to where or who the **Sacred** is, and as long as I can feel that Spirit, it's okay, don't you think?" As I opened the heavy wooden door and walked out into the Burggasse, I knew I was now ready to become Jewish. What enveloped my soul was that it wasn't religion that mattered, but the spirit of treating others the way you want to be treated. God would understand.

At my first meeting with the Jewish congregation in Straubing at Purimfest, I met a girl who was about my age. At first, I noticed her from a distance. She had red, curly hair and wore a delicate blue chiffon dress. The top was fitted, and the short skirt bounced each time she moved. I stood there in my thick flannel suit, light beige and grey plaid. My mother had it tailored for me, but I felt like an old housewife compared to the chiffon girl. How adorable she looked! With my thick hose, which creased around my knees and made my black patent leather shoes too tight, I just wanted to sink into the floor. This girl wore shiny nylon stockings that were as gauzy and thin as my mother's. What I would have given to look like that! Even in my school, no girl had clothes like that.

When the girl was introduced to me, I learned her name was Hanni. I mustered all my courage and asked, "Where did you get this beautiful dress from?"

She smiled and said, "It is from New York. My relatives live there, and they sent it to me."

New York! It seemed unattainable to me. How I would have liked to fly to my aunt in Canada, but not even that had worked out.

Twice a week now, I spent my time in a room in the synagogue on Wittelsbach Street preparing for my new faith. Before I entered each time, I stopped to look at the two towers and the large round glass window with the Star of David. For me, everything was different in the synagogue and the adjoining Hebrew school in the back. For one, there were boys in this class. Also, totally unlike my school, the teacher seemed to not raise an eyebrow when we all spoke at once, giggled with each other and laughed freely.

My parents and I celebrated a last Christmas with my uncle's family—with Midnight Mass, a Christmas tree, tinsel, bratwurst, potato salad, and gifts. I once again savored the smell of the fir tree, the hazelnut macaroons, the vanilla cookies, and the cinnamon and cloves from the mulled wine. I remembered the magical moments when we children were finally allowed to see the decorated Christmas tree, when we sang "Silent Night" in front of the countless flickering candles that looked like a sea of lights.

Those moments when my father joined happily in the singing are imprinted forever in my memory. I would have liked many more Christmases like that, but they could only happen in my thoughts.

At eleven years old, I converted. For several days the women of the Jewish community prepared my mother and me for our important day. Everything was under the supervision of the rabbi. In the mikveh, a ritual bath, we were to be cleansed from our impurities, be it mental or physical, by full immersion in water, which had to be "living water" from a spring, not the tap. I began to shake as I stood next to my mother in a pool filled with rainwater. We had to be immersed all the way, including our head and hair, and it felt icy cold.

After our hair was dry again, my parents celebrated a traditional wedding procession under the chuppah, the ceremonial wedding canopy. My mother walked around my father seven times and he put a wedding ring on her finger. Seven blessings were spoken for the bride and groom, and they both drank from a glass of wine. My father broke this glass with his right foot, and everyone shouted, "Mazel tov!"

I watched them and did not know if I should laugh or cry. The Jewish music that accompanied the ceremony was joyous and sad at the same time and suited my mood exactly. I was very happy for my father; a great wish had been fulfilled for him on that day. Even as a small boy, he had learned from his parents how important the wedding celebration is in Judaism. Over fifteen years after my parents' first wedding ceremony, they finally had the Jewish spiritual blessing—and we were now ready for the visit from Canada. The celebration in the Jewish community, with all the kosher food my parents had ordered coming from Munich and some of which they painstakingly prepared themselves, was high-spirited and relaxed. Everyone took us in warmly, embraced us and celebrated the day with us.

But I still felt as if I did not belong. To the Jewish people I seemed like the Bavarian and to the Bavarians I was the Jewish girl. Would I ever fit in anywhere?

At that time everything else around me changed too. My parents opened a newly renovated bigger shop on Schlesische Street, so they were able to get in many new items, from dumplings to red beets and preserves and canned food, to fresh foods stored in the new gigantic refrigerated counter. Every evening, they discussed with our staff what they wanted to present in the refrigeration display: there were over forty different cold cuts, all kinds of sausages, meat salads, schnitzel, steak, beef medallions and pork fillets. What I was most delighted about were the many flavors of ice cream we now sold. I was in charge of this, my favorite freezer, making sure we always had enough stock. This presented a new challenge to occupy me. Any opportunity to rise to an occasion was better than being bored and living in painful moments. I would not allow myself to dwell on missing the old store or my old room.

We had also moved from our old apartment to a more spacious one above the new store, and I had switched to the Ulrich Schmidl School in our new neighborhood. I was no longer in the nun's convent. Every morning I walked to school and from day one I was thrilled by my new teacher. Frau Spanner was very lively, and I loved listening to her in class. When she talked so animatedly about how Straubing's signature city tower was built as a watchtower in 1316, it all came alive to me. Through her stories, I was able to put myself in the shoes of the people of that time. I was impressed by the church windows she showed us and the filigree work done hundreds of years ago.

Through all of Grade Five and into Grade Six, I trusted my new teacher so much that I told her I had converted to Judaism and even why.

"Honestly, Elke," Frau Spanner said, "in my opinion, it was no coincidence that you and your father met this friend in Munich. I think this is the way it had to be."

I, who was still waiting to meet my aunt one day, answered, "I only wonder where all this leads."

"You'll sort it all out. I can well imagine that this was just a bit too much for you at once. But you'll find your way, of that I'm sure," she said, smiling. A few weeks later, after class, she brought me to the teacher's desk. She advised me to take an entrance exam for a middle school and higher education strand than I was currently in, even if it meant I would have to switch schools. This school offered a curriculum designed to prepare young women for business. The focus was on math, English, history and geography. It happened to be the only middle school in town, and again, it was led by nuns. My feelings about the nuns were mixed, based on two dramatically different experiences with Sister Michaela and Sister X.

I hoped for the best and wrote the entrance exam. At least it would be a step in the right direction of higher education. Unexpectedly, a couple of weeks later Frau Spanner appeared one day in our store. At first, I felt the same way I had when the Sister called my mother in for a meeting at the convent school. Had I made a mistake? Had I not passed the test? I was in the yard cleaning my bike when an apprentice came to get me. "Elke, come quickly, your teacher is in the shop."

Again, my heart was pounding out of my chest as I ran after him to find out what was happening.

Frau Spanner, tall and handsome in her Bavarian garb, always impressive, stood before the new counter and grinned at me. "Hello, Elke. I could not wait any longer. I got your results."

She reached into her leather case and took out a piece of paper. Quickly I glanced at the typewritten words but did not really understand what it meant. "You passed the exam very well. Every question has almost the highest possible score. Congratulations!"

She gave me a hug. "I'm sorry—it is too bad that I will not see you around the school in September. In any case I would not have been your classroom teacher in Grade Seven; I will start teaching the next Grade Five class. I hope we keep in touch!"

I felt the same way. But I still had until the end of the school year in her class, and I pushed these thoughts away. Also, Hanna had written us in her last letter that she and her family had booked a flight to Munich.

It had been twenty-seven years since my father and sister last saw each other. On the morning of her arrival, my father and I went to a flower shop. There, carefully and with trembling hands, he selected the twenty-seven most beautiful roses he could find. He paid close attention to choosing those with the longest stalks, pulling them out of the vases and comparing them with each other. He poured all his heart into selecting these roses—they were a symbol of his love and devotion to her, loaded with so much sadness at the same time. I watched very quietly as he closely inspected the petals and leaves for their fullness and freshness. I felt his pain and grief at what had been lost and what could have been in those twenty-seven years. I stood back to give him time.

With the enormous bouquet in his hand, my father stood next to me and my mother at the Munich airport that afternoon in the arrival hall. The letters and numbers rattled across the big billboards and finally indicated that the flight from Montreal had landed. It wouldn't be much longer. It had been twenty-seven years—and now these last few minutes seemed endless.

The door opened and the first passengers came through, with heavy suitcases on carts, carrying small children in their arms, waving at their relatives waiting for them. I stood on tiptoes behind the barrier and tried to remember exactly what my aunt looked like in the photo she had sent us.

My father looked at every single passenger. My mother's eyes followed a woman with black hair, then came to the conclusion that this was not my aunt. We were so busy looking that we did not notice that someone was calling us. Announcements were being made over the loudspeaker and new arrivals chatted next to us, telling their loved ones about their flight.

"Alex," I suddenly heard a hoarse voice. "Alex."

My father flinched and turned around to find her standing in front of him: his sister—my Aunt Hanna. She wore a tight dark blue skirt with matching fitted jacket and a white silk blouse. Her dark hair shimmered under the fluorescent lights of the arrival hall. She cried and spread her arms wide. My father pressed the bouquet into my mother's hands and rushed to his sister. Mom and I stopped and watched them as they hugged each other, as they sobbed. I heard no more announcements over the loudspeaker, no chattering of the passengers behind us, no rolling of the suitcase carts. I saw only my father and his sister. Tears ran down my cheeks onto my best, light-blue Lurex sweater, as I tried my best to smile.

After a few minutes that felt much longer, Hanna let go of my father and wanted to hug my mother, who stood as if paralyzed, not knowing what to do with the twenty-seven roses. Finally, she handed Hanna the bouquet. Hanna smiled as she held the roses and seemed even more touched. She closed her eyes and inhaled their scent. My father finally took the bouquet so she could properly greet my mother—crying and laughing, she came towards my mother and they embraced. Then Hanna came to me. "Elke," she whispered, and looked in my face. She brushed her fingers over my hair and face, as if to confirm that I was really standing in front of her. Rarely had I ever felt someone so warm, so loving toward me.

Hanna gave me a kiss on the cheek and beamed at me. The first excitement was over. Now my father was speaking in Yiddish and my mother and I in Bavarian with a few words of English to Hanna. Hanna's husband and two children stood a few meters away with the suitcases, watching us. Shyly, I looked at them and they smiled back.

My cousin Esther was five years younger than me. As she came toward me, her shining black hair swung with each step. She had pink cheeks and looked up at me with dark eyes. I could feel she was happy to see me. "Hello," she said, grinning.

My cousin Sollie was two years older than me, wearing bellbottom pants and a short-sleeved T-shirt. His hair was longer than that of the boys I knew, and I had never seen the kind of shoes he was wearing. I thought he looked really good. He shook my hand, tugged at the sleeve of my sweater, and pointed to the luggage with his finger. We laughed and I helped them carry the suitcases out of the hall. I was relieved that I understood what he wanted from me. Anything else would have been so embarrassing.

Soon, however, I realized that the little bit of English I learned at school wouldn't work for a conversation with my Canadian relatives. Hanna, her husband Henjek, and Sollie and Esther were staying at a hotel in the city square and we dropped them off there. When they came to our store and apartment the next morning, Sollie asked me something. I could only understand that it had something to do with keys. I had caught the word "key" and was quite excited that I had understood it. From school I happened to know the sentence: "Would you like the car key?" This was my opportunity to finally prove my knowledge of English. So I asked him again if he wanted the car key.

But he shook his head and repeated his question—again with the word "key" in it. "No, no, washroom. Waaaaaash-room." He said this last word several times, very slowly. He shrugged his shoulders—I realized he was annoyed and getting impatient. But I just simply did not know what "waaaaashroom" meant.

"Where is the car key?" was another sentence I had just learned at school. Maybe that would calm him down. So I asked my cousin where the car key was. He looked at me wide eyed and jumped up from his chair. I realized he didn't know what to do. He seemed worried. Then he tried desperately to use his hands, pointing and trying to show me something. I was disappointed in myself, because I simply did not understand what he wanted. Now I had the feeling that it was a dire situation, and I ran to my aunt. A short time later, with translation aid from Hanna and my father, it became clear: Sollie wanted to go the toilet and thought he needed a key to unlock and lock it.

I was ashamed. I should have known. At last my relatives from Canada were here, and I hoped they were not too disappointed in me. You just have to learn better English, I admonished myself. This gave me hope that I had not destroyed their love for me right on the very first day.

On our first evening together, I unwrapped the gift they had brought me from Montreal: sky-blue capris. From then on, I wore them every day, mostly with a white T-shirt, and felt like a part of my Canadian family. This was the best way I knew to show my love for them.

Everything that had been lost in twenty-seven years had to be packed into those two weeks, every moment was important and laden with bittersweet emotions. It seemed impossible to even make a dent in catching up with what had been lost. And before we knew it, they were leaving again.

On one of the last afternoons, my Aunt Hanna told us that we should go to the yard to play. "The adults have to talk to each other now," she said, sounding strict for the first time in these two weeks. Aunt Hanna had waited a long time for the right moment, but it just hadn't happened. So, she decided to tell my father just before her departure what she had been putting off saying since her arrival.

My father now learned something that he would never have thought possible: his father Arye had never arrived in the concentration camp in the summer of 1940. He had told his wife and Hanna he was going to find a way to protect his family. He was looking for an opportunity to jump off the train and find a way to get his family back. Arye managed to return to the farm near Wieluń, fetched the rest of the jewelry and the gold he had hidden there, which had not been found by the Gestapo, and had gone to a farmer in the neighborhood. Hanna had investigated this and found out that Arye had given the farmer everything he had, in the hope that he would help hide him and find a way to get his family back.

But these farmers were not the Pichlhubers. They had betrayed Arye and given him up to a troop of SS men. Arye was executed on a dirt road not far from his farm.

After the war, Hanna had tried to find out who the farmer was who had denounced their father and what had happened to all the land, jewelry and their family's money. But she did not get far with her inquiries. She was shut down, their entire estate had been lost, and the Polish government had built a school on the former grounds.

Chapter 11

The secret boyfriend

Straubing, 1968

After Hanna left with her family, my life felt empty. Nothing fit together anymore. I was now in a different school in the city. It was a higher education, the only business-oriented middle school in town, but not the one Sister Michaela had outlined for me in Grade Two. Plans for me to go to the Gymnasium, the highest type of education leading to university, had been pushed aside with the excitement of our visitors from Canada, our move and the new shop. I often thought about bringing up the Gymnasium again with my parents—but the right moment just never came. Somehow, everything seemed too much already, and I did not want to burden my parents even more.

I always tried to keep any difficulties away from my parents. This responsibility was far more pronounced in me than in any of the other children around me. Later, I read books on children with parents who survived the Holocaust, and one of them described my situation exactly. I was constantly trying to compensate for and help relieve the pain my father had suffered in his childhood and youth. Being an empathetic child, his pain was palpable to me: I could feel how much the loss of his former life, the shame and the humiliation he endured, still persecuted him. How could I think of myself and push for the highest education when there were such everyday struggles?

Life then was always incredibly busy, always something to be done. Goods to be ordered, the display cleaned, cold cuts had to be arranged on beautiful platters as part of the catering we did. Just as I felt in the Jewish community—not really belonging—that's how I felt at the convent middle school. Now I was separated from the other girls during the religious education. I was constantly admonished by the nuns about my skirts, which in their eyes seemed much too short. They had many rules I simply could not understand.

I was frightened of one nun in particular—the math teacher. I was fine with the subject but her screaming fits were unbearable to me. Everyone knew that if she ever saw a student with a boy on the street, that girl would surely be called to the blackboard to solve a particularly difficult problem. Then the nun would proceed to humiliate the student in front of everyone. She screamed insults at them about being stupid and boy crazy.

"Why can't we do both, live a little and do well at school?" I wanted to scream at her. By that time, I had experienced some good teachers, and her mean-spirited put-downs were intolerable to me. I lost my enthusiasm for school.

My only distraction was my school friends. In the morning I met two of them, both named Ingrid, and we biked together to school. In the pouring rain, we held an umbrella in one hand and steered with the other. In the snow, we had to be careful not to slip, but it was still a lot more fun than taking the bus.

Every now and then I met one of my Jewish friends after school. We never tired of listening to Scott McKenzie sing, "If you're going to San Francisco" all afternoon. We tried to translate the words, then went into the garden, picked a few flowers and put them in our hair. We dreamed of being somewhere other than Straubing, linked hands and danced together. When I saw pictures of San Francisco in the newspaper or on television, I soaked them up. In the evening in my bed, I imagined myself there, living like the hippies—with long hair, embroidered blouses and fur jackets, completely free and without any stupid clothing regulations.

One morning, my father woke up with facial paralysis. A corner of his mouth and an eyelid hung down limp and motionless. As much as he tried, he could not move his face normally. The doctor examined him a few hours later but could not detect any signs of a stroke. Perhaps, with the new shop and apartment and his sister, everything had become too much for him.

Later, I was certain his dark emotions and memories had come back in full force. The ghosts from the past, as they say.

It was clear that he had to slow down and the doctor wanted to send him away for a break to a rehabilitation spa. There, they wanted to restore him with mineral baths and absolute calm. The first days, however, he was to stay in bed at home and recover. He could not stand this, and he came to the store, but the reactions of the customers shocked him so much that he locked himself in the apartment for a few hours. Most people were horrified when they saw him, and immediately asked what had happened and whether there was a chance for a cure. He realized how bad he looked and how important it was for him to try whatever he could to get well again. I imagine he also felt that my mother and I did not know how to deal with him. If we tried to gloss over it, we felt bad and uncaring; if we talked to him or asked about something, he said we could not understand because of his slurred speech and became angry. We were all sad.

After my father had woken up with the paralysis, I noticed my mother could not cope alone in the big new shop. She worked twice as hard as usual, but she had only been in the meat production area occasionally, when my father had to be elsewhere. She had never ordered goods from the livestock traders, who wanted to speak only to my father. How could she cope with everything? I recognized immediately that I had to intervene somehow.

For me, one thing led to another. My parents would need me in the shop more than ever. In the school, on the other hand, my friends would be able to get on without me. I began to make my decision—I would stop going to school to help my parents. My mother, I thought, had so far not dared to ask me, and was probably waiting for me to finally offer.

One afternoon I came home from school and waited in the room next to the store until my mother had locked the shop. I heard the lock and then her steps on the tile floor. She opened the door, sat down at the table, and drank a glass of water.

"Mama," I said tentatively. "Mama, do you have time?"

My mother put the glass down and looked at me seriously. She probably thought I would confess something to her because I had gotten into trouble.

"Mama, what do you think about me starting work in the shop?" I tried to interpret from her expression how she was taking it. But she remained still and looked at me.

"I, uh, I could work here in the shop, as an apprentice." I knew all the apprentices my parents had taken on. I had gone along to meet them when my parents visited them at home in their villages in the country or the Bavarian Forest. My parents interviewed them and asked me, although I was still a young girl, what I thought of them. They had always appreciated my advice. Generally, my perceptions about the new employees seemed correct and they had proved their worth. That gave me courage. I knew what to look for, so why could I not be an apprentice myself?

"You know, I can learn something from you and earn a little money ..." I didn't take my eyes off her. Would she get angry? Would she beseech me not to break off school? Would she hug me with relief? At that moment, I really had no idea.

Just as I wanted to get going with other arguments, she said, "Elke, I agree." She breathed deeply. I felt that she was relieved. "You'll do a regular apprenticeship, and I know I can rely on you. It would help me a lot," she said and smiled. "This way, you can look at the business and decide if you want to take it over later. I promise you do not have to go to the slaughterhouse. And if you do not like it here, you'll just go back to school."

So, at fourteen, I started my first job, in the shop of my parents.

Saturday was the busiest day of the week as we closed early and the stores were closed on Sundays. Many customers preferred to pre-order in advance, so they did not have to wait a long time in the shop when it was full of people. This was very time-consuming for us and the orders had to be all done before the store opened. At four o'clock, Saturday morning, my father knocked on my bedroom door. "Time to get up," he shouted, "We'll start in fifteen minutes." I hoped I had misheard. The down blanket felt soft and warm and I did not want to get up and rush across the yard in the cold. So, I turned on my side and cuddled into the pillow. But it did not help. I had to get up right away or I would fall asleep again. I groped around my room in the dark but could not find my bathrobe or my slippers. Next time put things right next to your bed, I told myself in a half-sleep.

Ten minutes later I was in the shop. The apprentices pulled fresh cold cuts out of the refrigerator to put in the refrigerated display counter and my mother checked the orders for the day and laid them out for us.

We apprentices had to go through the adjoining room, out into the dark and across the yard into the meat production area to bring in heavy steel trays laden with sausages and meat for the special orders.

I opened the heavy door and the smell of ground beef wafted over from the butchers. It was half past four in the morning. The butcher and apprentices hustled about. Long chains of sausages lay on the worktops and there was a lot of banging and shouting. I held my breath and hurried to the cold store, unlocked the door, and had to squeeze my eyes shut against the cold. I tried to lift the trays covered

with sausages, but they felt like they would pull my arms out of the sockets. But of course, I said nothing.
When the pre-orders were finally finished, the display filled and the cash register prepared, I was able to take a quick break in the adjoining room before we opened the store. It was light outside now, and my father stood by the window, looking out, rocking back and forth. I could see the drooping corner of his mouth in profile. It seemed as if he was moving to music, but it was totally quiet in the room. I asked him if I should turn on the radio. I wanted to change the strange situation.

"You know, Elke, most people do not know who they are," he whispered to the window without looking at me.

"How? What do you mean?"

"Only today I had to think of him again. I had made a friend in that horrible place and they just killed him." He stared straight ahead, motionless.

"What are you talking about? You never talk about that time."

Then he told me the story of the quarry in Mauthausen and how the SS had shot his friend. How they had pounded stones in the blazing sun, how they had begged for water, how afraid they'd been of falling from weakness.

Then he turned to me. I was frightened. His face was chalk-white and distorted by the paralysis. Beads of sweat ran down his temples.

"I would have loved to at least give him a proper burial," he said, and sobbed, his eyes glazing over. "But they threw him into a pit, like rubbish."

I searched for the right thing to say and tried to nod understandingly.

"If only I could help him." He closed his eyes, deep creases forming on his forehead. I did not know what to do. Suddenly, he opened his eyes and his voice grew louder: "And now? Now I'm useless again!" For him, the facial paralysis brought back all sorts of feelings of helplessness and anger over what was happening to him. He was flooded by feelings of powerlessness. He struggled for control, but to his horror it eluded him. His body shook and trembled uncontrollably.

"But Dad ..." I stroked his shoulder, a helpless attempt to comfort him and ease his shaking.

"I cannot even help you in the shop, because the customers are frightened by me. I just have to find a way to get on my feet again. You need me, the store needs me. I do not want to fail again. I do not want to fail you."

Even though the corner of his mouth still drooped unchanged, his facial expression now seemed determined and his body started to calm. And just like that he found the fighter in him again.

And this time he was not alone. He had me and my mother. We were there to help.

As apprentices we also learned to cut thin slices of cold cuts on the machine without slicing our fingers; estimate how to cut a piece of liver sausage so it would weigh the amount requested; add sums in our minds and know how much money the customer should get back. Good service was very important and every customer was treated kindly. In addition, we were responsible for keeping the store clean; the glass of the display counter should shine, the tile floor needed to be spotless, no fingerprints could show on the glass entrance door. During the day, the display needed to be filled with appetizing cold cuts; in the evening, any unsold items had to be put back into the colder refrigerators for optimum freshness. Only after my parents checked and approved that everything was in order did the other apprentices and I finally have some free time. During the week, that was around 7:00 p.m. The only thing I could do then was to chat or play games with the apprentices who had their own room in our building. On Saturday afternoon, the apprentices drove home to their families and stayed there until Sunday evening—on that day they were free, as was I.

For me, there was only one way out of all the sadness and gloom in the shop: music, parties and dancing. When I was invited to my very first party at fourteen, I was so excited I could not sleep the night before. I doubted that my father would let me go, but Bernard, the boy who threw the party, was part of the Jewish community. He was four years older than me, and normally I would not have associated with such older boys. But since there were only ten Jewish families in Straubing and only three boys within a few years of my age, it was slim pickings and my father knew and liked Bernard.

My dad was keen for me to make new friends within the Jewish community. I also sensed he wanted to prevent me developing attachments to German boys. Since I'd converted to Judaism and he could see I was turning into a teenager, the worry about German boys was mounting. The pressure in the Jewish community, even in this small Straubing community, was to date within the faith. Despite these pressures my newly converted mother empathized with my need to socialize with whomever I liked. I had already confessed to her how hard the days were for me—the heavy lifting in the cold storage, the early rising, my father's illness. I'd even trusted her enough to say I was thinking of running away.

Her surprising answer was, "I would not blame you, Elke. Can I come with you?" But of course, she stayed in the store and supported my father wherever she could. My mom was stuck in the middle between the two of us. She was worried my dad's condition would worsen, and he could have a heart attack on top of the facial paralysis, if faced with too much upset. So, she resolved that it was best he didn't know it was a party that included mostly German teenagers from Bernard's school. She felt I needed to get out and have some fun. Since she needed to lend me her support in secrecy, the complicated scenario was wrought with difficulties for all of us.

On that particular Saturday, I begged my father to let me go to Bernard's party. I sold it to him as an evening for the youths of our Jewish community. Whether he knew I was fibbing, I cannot say, but he actually let me go. My mother lent me her soft pink lipstick, and I realized how proud she was when she first saw me in the mini dress we'd bought in the city. The delicate pink and white batik pattern was all the rage, and I was pleased to see the lipstick matched perfectly. Finally, I slipped into white Roman sandals and laced them over my calves. A last look in the mirror and I was ready.

My mother drove me to the entrance at Spitalgasse where an illuminated "Taverne" sign glimmered over the door. I opened the car door and heard the bass of the music. Slowly I went to the tavern door and peered down the stairs. It seemed to be totally dark and I smelled the cigarette smoke. I felt completely different than at home. I was insecure. I had imagined all this so differently. I crept down the stairs cautiously, the music and laughter growing louder with each step. I stood at the front of a huge, dark room with vaulted ceilings. Everywhere, people sat on dark wooden furniture, chatting and drinking. The smoke hung above us like a cloud. I felt like an extraterrestrial. Many young people, all at least four years older than me, crowded on the dance floor, talking, smoking and clinking their drinks, as music buzzed from big speakers. I knew I was much too young and felt like a little girl who did not belong there at all. How embarrassing! I wished I had known what this would be like. For a moment, I thought to turn quickly and run up the stairs. Perhaps no one had seen me—my mother was still waiting nearby.

But too late. Bernard had seen me and called from the bar. "Hey, Elke! Come here!"

I slipped past all the people. Some smiled at me, some looked me over skeptically. Bernard leaned casually at the bar, sipping his beer and talking to another young man. Shyly, I greeted Bernard, trying to pretend I had been going to this kind of parties all my life. As I spoke to him, I noticed that the other young man was watching me. He grinned. Should I pretend not to notice him? As I thought about it, he reached out his hand to shake my hand. "Hi, I'm Franz. What's your name?" He was much taller than me, handsome, with chin-length blond hair, and the clearest blue eyes I had ever seen.

I almost began to stutter. But I managed to say my name and smile.

"What do you like to drink?" he asked. Since it was my first party ever, I had no idea what people ordered in a discotheque.

"Oh, something ..." I replied, and shrugged, hoping to come across as a bit daring and mature.

"I'll get you something. Do not move from this spot. I'll be right back." He turned and hurried along the bar.

While he was gone, I watched Bernard. He whispered something into the ear of a young woman with long, dark hair. She laughed loudly and stroked his cheek. I thought I'd seen her before with him. She probably was a classmate, like most of the young people here. Only, I was no longer at school, but wrapped sausages in wax paper all day. I realized again how differently things could have gone.

Before I could brood further, Franz stood in front of me with a glass of dark red liquid. "Here," he said, "there is not much alcohol in this." I sipped it. The alcohol burned in my mouth and throat and tasted like sharp toothpaste.

"Tastes good," I whispered, grinning at him. Since I had not the slightest idea what to talk to him about, I simply sipped my drink and looked around.

"Do you like this song?" he asked me suddenly.

The last gulp stuck in my throat. I cleared it and said, "Oh, yes, "Love is All You Need" is one of my favorite songs! The Beatles are just amazing." I was proud to know the song and be able to tell him which band it was. Just as "The Marseillaise" finished at the beginning of the song, he grabbed my hand and pulled me behind him to the dance floor. We pushed past all the couples and stopped in the middle of the dance floor. As I had with "Charlie Brown," I began to move to the rhythm of the music.

I had practiced dancing secretly in my room in front of the mirror. I knew very well that my father did not want to see me dancing around to this kind of music. He could forbid me to do it in the living room, but not in my own room. When I had the feeling I had gotten a bit too wild and made my father aware of me, I laid down on my bed with my eyes closed, just listening to the lyrics.

Everything I had practiced at home now flowed out of me quite naturally.

I loved every kind of new music, from the twist to rock 'n' roll. Even more, I loved the freedom the music gave me. When I moved to the beat, I forgot the fingerprints on the glass door, the blood-stained oil cloth aprons of the butchers, and my father's illness.

"Love, love, love ..." I had not noticed that Franz had tried to put his hands on my hips. He could not hold me now; nothing could hold me back. Until the first notes of "A Whiter Shade of Pale" played—then something happened that I had never experienced before. Franz drew me close, putting one arm around my back and the other over my shoulder.

I pressed my face to his cotton T-shirt and held on to his leather belt. With the other hand, I brushed his back. How can anybody possibly breathe like this? I thought. I turned my head away from his chest to see how the other girls managed. They seemed relaxed. One of them had her eyes closed and smiled quite happily. Franz had probably noticed that I was looking around. He put his fingers to my chin and lifted my head up so I looked him straight in the eyes.

"I just want to be with you," he whispered.

What is going on with me? I thought. I felt hot and cold at the same time. My knees shook and for some reason I was not listening to the song anymore. I had forgotten everything around me as I smiled up at him. Then he pressed me to him tightly again and stroked my back. I felt a tingling in my stomach. Was it what the older apprentices sometimes whispered about? Then I realized I would never have experienced this feeling as a nun and had to smile.

For the rest of the evening, I worried no more about talking and just danced.

I opened my eyes again after another slow song, "Je t'aime," and looked at my watch.

"I have to go now," I told Franz. My mother would be waiting outside.

"When will we meet again?" he asked, holding my hands.

"I, uh, I do not think that's possible," I stammered. "I was only allowed to come because a boy from the Jewish community invited me."

He clearly was not happy with that answer, I could tell.

"My father will not allow me to go to anyone else's party," I added.

For a short while we both said nothing.

"The guy who invited you, Bernard, he is my friend. I often go to the public swimming pool with him and some others. Maybe you are allowed to go there? Wouldn't your father say yes if you went swimming?"

I thought about it briefly. In fact, my father might agree to that. I did not have to mention that Franz would be there. Maybe Mom would help me with the cover-up. So I said, "All right. Then let's go to the outdoor pool next weekend."

I could hardly wait to finish my work on the Saturday. I had been on my feet since 4:00 a.m., constantly lifting, cutting, being friendly to every customer and trying to give them the correct change. I now stood behind the counter, peering over it to watch the last few customers as they unhurriedly packed their paper-wrapped cold cuts, wieners and bratwurst into bags and baskets. Nervously, I tapped my fingers on the counter and stole surreptitious looks at my wristwatch. My mother would never let me close the store early, that was for sure. It didn't matter to her if the weather was nice or if the apprentices wanted to leave as quickly as possible. The most important thing to her was that the customers were happy. That is why she continued chatting with an older woman while already holding the keys to the door in her hand.

This was my signal, along with the other apprentices. I put the leftover sausages, flanks of beef and schnitzel in the cold storage. It took at least an hour until everything was scrubbed and clean. I looked at my watch a few more times. The others have already been at the outdoor swimming pool since noon, I thought to myself as I washed the aluminum platters in the kitchen sink. Hopefully they are still there. Hopefully Franz is still there.

At three o'clock, I finally finished. I hastily left the store and ran through the adjoining room out into the hall and up the two flights of stairs to our apartment. Once I was in my room, I peeked out the window and was relieved to see no storm clouds brewing. I jumped in the shower to remove the smell of meatloaf and salami, slipped into my new red bikini and threw a light summer dress over it. To my parents, who were in the apartment by now, I called out, "I'm off! I'll be back around nine or sooo!" I slammed the door behind me, flew down the stairs into the basement and dragged my bike upstairs. I swung into the saddle and pedaled for all I was worth.

The bike ride from the east of Straubing to the outdoor swimming pool in the south took half an hour at the most. The air shimmered over tar that had been baked by the sun all day. I pushed the pedals until sweat ran down my face and back. Faster, faster, I cheered myself on. On one street, children were playing with a ball. An older boy had grabbed a garden hose and was spraying it into the street. I cycled under the spray and smelled that peculiar mixture you only get at the height of summer when water evaporates on tar. Finally, something other than the smell of sausage water, I thought to myself.

By the entrance to the grounds for the public swimming pool, I locked up my bike. While I ran toward the entrance, I counted the exact change for the admission fee. My first stop was the bathroom. I had to wipe the sweat off my face and fix my hair. My hands were shaky from the fast trip and excitement.

I forced myself to walk slowly to where my friends were lying on their blankets. I didn't want anyone to know how I had raced to get there. They were lounging on their towels and blankets, licking ice cream, smoking cigarettes, playing cards and laughing. And of course, Franz was still there.

Franz and I laid side by side on a blanket and secretly held hands. My arm had almost fallen asleep, but I didn't dare move because I didn't want him to let go. Even though our friends sat around us, and most likely none of the other pool visitors would have noticed, I had an uneasy feeling the whole time. What if someone saw us? What if someone told my father? But this fear didn't stop me from meeting Franz at the pool again.

And it continued that way for weeks. I hoped every weekend that no thunderstorm would come up—whether in the form of bad weather or my dad getting wind of the situation. At some point, Franz whispered to me that perhaps we should meet somewhere else, where there weren't so many other people around. How did he envision this happening? Just meeting him at the swimming pool was already a risk. And on top of that, I practically had no free time during the week.

Just as I was going to say it would never work, I thought of the Hebrew classes in the synagogue. I could ask my father to pick me up a little later. Then I would have a short time to see Franz. If I asked for more time, my dad would be suspicious. I could make it ten minutes at the most, I thought to myself, but ten minutes are better than none.

So, Franz and I arranged our first rendezvous, in the bushes behind the synagogue.

Halfway through the Hebrew class I stopped listening to the rabbi as I ran through scenarios in my mind, over and over. I imagined how I would race out of the room before anyone else, how I would manage it so that no one would notice us hiding behind the synagogue, and how I would make it to where my father sat with his car running in front of the synagogue. A few minutes before the hour was finally over, I mumbled an apology to the rabbi and rushed down the stairs and out the side entrance into the yard before everyone else.

There stood Franz, waiting for me, looking uncertain. If he was feeling unsure, the feeling was multiplied a million times for me. My mind was in turmoil. I had to act quickly. First, I looked around—no one was in sight. "*Pssst*," I hissed at him, and held my index finger over my lips. "Come, hurry! We have to get behind the synagogue before the others arrive!" I whispered.

We held hands and ran around the corner of the building. There I leaned against the building, and we both took a deep breath. Then another horrible thought entered my mind. What would happen if someone came to smoke behind the synagogue? Would they catch us right away? No, that just can't be, I tried to convince myself.

The first minutes alone with Franz felt like an eternity because when you have the feeling you will be caught at any moment, everything seems to happen in slow motion. I turned my head and looked in the direction of the building corner over and over. Would someone peer around the corner at us? At the same time, I had only one wish—that he would just kiss me. Finally, I closed my eyes. Kiss me now, I thought to myself, resisting the urge to look at my watch. Hopefully, my father was not in front of the synagogue with the car already. What if he didn't remember we were meeting ten minutes later?

I was so agitated that I opened my eyes again. Franz looked at me. We stood like that for a while until he pulled me close and our lips touched. My first kiss felt gentle, not wet or uncomfortable. Franz's skin tasted fresh, just like his breath. Again, I felt that tickle in my stomach, just like on the dance floor in the tavern. If only we hadn't been just standing behind the synagogue. If only I hadn't been thinking of my father, the whole time.

The Taverne also offered dancing on Sunday afternoon, and Franz and I decided to meet there. I told my dad I was meeting friends. My conscience troubled me, of course. What would happen if he found out I had a German boyfriend?

My father never asked, but I had the feeling he could tell something was up. There were days we didn't speak a single word to each other. When I said goodbye to my parents in the living room on Sunday afternoons, I wore a long coat. Underneath was my mini dress. Only my mother knew about the dress. She knew I wanted to go dancing and she didn't want to take those few hours of fun away from me.

From the moment Franz and I were on the dance floor, letting ourselves be carried away by "Jumpin' Jack Flash," it was all worth it. It didn't seem to matter that someone might notice us and betray me. But that is exactly what happened.

When I came home one Sunday evening, my father was waiting for me at the door. His face was bright red, a big crease between his eyebrows. Something had happened, that much was clear. Quickly, I buttoned my long coat over my mini dress.

"Come in here immediately!" he barked, rushing into the living room. There he stopped and began screaming at me, "I know everything! I know that you were in a tavern kissing a boy!"

My heart beat faster. My knees began to shake. It had actually happened; we had been discovered.

"The daughter of Frau Müller told me everything, everything!" he roared. "This is terrible! This is unbelievable. My daughter doing such a thing!"

Tears welled up into my eyes. I would have liked to tell him how much I loved him, and that he should understand that everything was completely harmless; that we had only kissed a few times. But I couldn't say a single word. I swallowed and wiped my hands over my cheeks. Then I started to cry and the stress I had been carrying around for months came rushing out.

I screamed back, "Just leave me alone! I work here every day—can't I have even a few hours on Sundays to enjoy myself?"

"Are you crazy? You are much too young for such things. I will tell you one thing, you will never meet this boy again. Do you understand me?" His voice echoed throughout the living room. Never had he screamed so loud. "I don't care what you think. You will never, ever see him again!"

"You are overreacting. It was nothing!" I shot back. I was not even frightened now, but defiant. It was too late anyway. "I don't see it like that. I am going to do what I want!" I glared at him in anger.

We were both equally furious! Nevertheless, I did notice that the half of his face that was paralyzed seemed to sink lower. Maybe I was only imagining it, but it scared me and gave me a bad conscience. What if he had a stroke just because of me? What if he got worse? The living room was quiet again. We stood in front of each other without saying a word. I turned around, ran to my room and locked the door.

There I threw myself on my bed and tried to breathe deeply. Tears rolled down my cheeks and I felt my pulse throbbing. It was over. I would never be able to see Franz again.

Even though I knew I wouldn't be able to convince my father, I would have liked to talk to him about it. I would have liked to ask him why he couldn't be happy for me. In the evening, while in bed, I imagined all the things I could have said to him: You were saved by two German farmers—not all Germans are bad, right? I know that you like many Germans. You even say that yourself.

There was this one thing my father had drummed into my head since childhood: "Elke, there are good and bad people everywhere, among the Poles, the Germans and the Jews. You just have to be able to assess them properly."

Why did this idea suddenly not mean anything anymore? Did it apply only to him? I didn't understand anything anymore. I was not allowed to like Franz just because he wasn't Jewish? And for being too young? If I could handle the store, I could go out and handle myself.

But this conversation took place only in my thoughts. Maybe it was better that way: to bury those feelings in silence. Emotional outbursts were bad for him. They brought up too many dark memories and emotions—the ghosts of his past.

This is me at 14, ready to sneak out and go dancing.

Chapter 12

The decision
Travels in Europe and North America

1968–1975

After our big fight, we settled into an angry silence. The discomfort of it made me want to get out, get away from home even more. I would have loved to move out, but I was still fourteen. I couldn't think of a way to look after myself. I would still be dependent on my parents. So, I stayed.

My life ran like clockwork. Monday to Friday I got up every morning at 6:00 a.m. and helped prepare the store with the other apprentices. Once a week, on Tuesdays, I was allowed to go to the vocational school for the whole day, which I really looked forward to. This school delivered a certificate at the end of the sales apprenticeship. However, I realized quickly that the deli profession was not going to be for me once the apprenticeship would be finished. I discussed with my mother that I had found a way to complete the education I would have had with the nuns. In order to accomplish this next step, I needed to start attending a secondary school one night a week and a full Saturday while I was still doing my apprenticeship in the store.

I was determined to do it all and wasn't going to let my dad stop me. My mom had now become my spokesperson. She related the conversation about my continued education to my dad, and he was silent about it, at least to me. Which meant he pretended he did not notice how much I was pulling away from home. I pretended not to hear his disapproval in the silence.

The secondary school for continued education was located in the same building as the vocational school and I started classes there as soon as possible. This meant more distance between me and the store, as I spent every Wednesday night and all Saturday there.

I could hardly wait until I was finally at the bus stop, where I waited for the bus that took me to the school in the center of town. It was the same bus stop where I used to say goodbye to my grandfather when he visited us on Sundays. There, he often kissed my cheek and told me he was looking forward to reading to me from *Struwwelpeter*. Then he would laugh, climb into the bus, and wave at me through the window. I would stand there until I could not see the bus any longer.

It all seemed so long ago. Often, I squeezed my eyes tight and tried to imagine his face. I tried to remember his voice, his smell. Then I would hear the rattle of the engine and the hissing of the brakes, as the bus stopped, and the doors opened. I stepped in and was finally away from home for a few hours.

I had often been afraid of school in the past, but now it was just the opposite. My time at school was—besides dancing—my favorite time of the whole week. My escape, my luxury. This was not only because of the lessons. While the bus made its way down Schlesische Street towards the city, I looked forward to seeing my friends, especially one particular friend.

I straightened my dress and took a quick peek in my small pocket mirror to make sure my pink lipstick hadn't smeared. When the bus stopped in front of the school, my heart pounded just like at the entrance of the swimming pool. When the bus doors opened with a loud *pfffff*, I looked to see if he happened to be standing in front of the school. I recognized Richard at once, with his long, fringed brown hair, bellbottoms and turtleneck sweater. He smiled over at me. I grinned and went into the school building, trying hard not to fall up the stairs or do anything else embarrassing in my excitement. Now I would have to calm down before the lessons started, as he sat just a few seats over from me in the classroom.

I had been watching him since the very first Saturday of classes. He seemed so self-assured as he leaned back with his legs crossed nonchalantly and occasionally made notes. I liked him—his smile, his voice. Did he like me too? I was not sure. At least he had grinned at me before school; that was something. So, on this Saturday, just like always, I unpacked my notebooks and pens, put them on the table and vowed not to look over at him at all.

Slowly the other students trickled in. As is appropriate for the coolest guy in class, he came in last, a few minutes after the bell. The teacher gave him a brief stern look, which didn't seem to bother him at all, and the lessons began.

Just before the end of class, with my head resting on my hands, I was thinking that I would have to help my mother in the store with the checkout. Our teacher said, "We are going to have to clarify something else before we leave today. You have to vote for a class representative."

Richard casually raised his right hand. I woke up from my thoughts and looked at him.

"Yes, what is it?" the teacher said. You could tell by his voice that Richard was not exactly his favorite student.

"How about Elke?" Richard said, and looked at me. I think my heart stopped at that moment and my face felt red-hot. I flinched. What? What was he saying? I must have misunderstood.

"I mean, she gets along well with everyone, with us and the teachers. She would be exactly the right person." I swallowed and my mouth was dry.

The other students nodded, and the teacher came to my table. "Elke, do you want to be nominated in this election?" I stammered, "Ah, er, yeah ..."

They actually voted for me and from then on, I was the class representative. Then the bell rang. I had experienced the last few minutes as if in a trance and felt quite dizzy. He must like me, or he wouldn't have recommended me, I thought. But I didn't want to read too much into it and tried to collect myself. When I was ready to leave the classroom, Richard nudged me.

"I knew the others would choose you," he said, grinning. "Do you want to go to Venezia with me? For a panini?"

Again, I could only choke out an "Ah, er, yes." This was all just a bit too much at once. The only thing I was not thinking about at that moment was my father and all of his stupid rules. I could not care about that right then.

We slowly strolled together towards Venezia, the Italian ice cream and panini parlor where all the cool young people hung out. Richard went ahead, holding the glass door open. He nodded and smiled at me and I went in first. A couple of people standing by the counter looked over at me. I knew some of them from school. I was proud to come here with Richard, undoubtedly the coolest boy in class. Some of the girls looked a bit envious. We sat down at a kidney-shaped table and ordered a panini. I was so excited that I barely tasted the grilled cheese sandwich. I was busy focusing on Richard and seeing who else was there.

Finally, Richard flagged the waiter and requested a banana split "with two spoons." We ate this together, and it was definitely the most delicious banana split I had ever eaten.

In the evenings, as I lay in bed listening to my music cassette tapes, I was already looking forward to school on Saturday, and especially the hours afterwards with Richard in Venezia. As "Morning Has Broken" played, I closed my eyes and imagined what a future with Richard could look like. I wished that we could walk across the city square holding hands like a normal couple. But what if my father or someone else saw us? Would they betray us? Sometimes I imagined that Richard was sitting at a table with my parents. We would eat, have a conversation and laugh.

The situation seemed hopeless. The initial euphoria had given way to fear of being caught. Fear hung over everything I did. As much as I enjoyed my time with Richard, the hours afterwards were unbearable. Lying in bed wrestling with my thoughts, wondering what would happen. The situation with Richard would not end well, even though I was so in love with him. Maybe that was why I liked the songs "Leaving on a Jet Plane" and "Daydream Believer."

When I wrote down the lyrics and translated them line by line with my German-English dictionary, I noticed that these songs matched my life. I cranked up the volume on the Beatles, the Stones and the Bee Gees and danced around my room. I felt free and happy only in these moments. Then I remembered: I could never really be with Richard, as my father would do anything to prevent it. I crawled under the covers and listened to songs by Leonard Cohen and "Sad Lisa" by Cat Stevens. Often, I cried or just stared into space. Every time Cat Stevens sang the last verse about there must be more he could tell her, I wondered what that could be. What more could there be for me now? Was this it? Working every day at the store on Schlesische Street, wrestling flanks of meat into steel trays in the cold storage and finally, at some point, marrying someone my father approved of?

Since our fight over Franz, my father and I had hardly spoken. We communicated only the most vital things, mostly to do with the shop, until one evening toward the end of November.

I had taken my bike to school, as it was easier than taking the bus. By the time school was done for the day, a very thick fog had moved in. When I looked out the window, I could not see anything and on top of that, it was pitch black. We also had a longer discussion in class and talked about the exams. I knew it was late but had no choice but to get on my bike and make my way home. My little front bike light had little effect on the fog. It took forever to get home as I had to move very slowly, my hair becoming steadily damper.

When I unlocked the door to my parents' apartment, my father was already standing directly behind it. "Oh, how good that you are here!" he said, hugging me. He squeezed me tightly and suddenly began crying. He was trembling all over. "Elke, I thought something had happened to you ..."

For such a long time, I had longed for his understanding. I had missed his affection and his warmth so much. Now my tears flowed with his. How could it have gone so far that we had not talked to each other for months? I no longer felt the rage I had felt towards him, then suddenly, I wasn't afraid of him anymore. Why should I be? He was so fragile, so loving and so concerned about me. Arm in arm we walked to the living room and sat on the couch.

That was the evening my father told me how he had escaped from the Ganacker concentration camp as a young man.

I heard about the night he spent under the dead bodies and the thoughts he had while there. If you hear such stories from someone who is close to you, you experience it yourself, and you suffer along with them. You can feel the fear, the pain and the horror.

That night I couldn't sleep. I imagined how my father, a defenseless child, had been handed over to the SS and how he had survived that last night in the concentration camp. I had the images in my mind of the photos the Americans had taken when they liberated the concentration camps. I saw mountains of countless emaciated naked corpses before me—and knew my father had had to hide in a mountain like that. I thought my head would burst.

For that brief moment on the sofa in our living room, we were close again—father and daughter—speaking to one another. But what followed, the images and thoughts that haunted me, were even worse than not speaking to one another. Sometimes a dam bursts wide open and all that suppressed emotion comes gushing out, and we both were flooded by that emotional current. Neither of us knew what to do with the confusing overwhelm of loss. We silently agreed to close the dam again. At least that way we could function, each lost in our own positions on how to carve a life in this world. The next morning, we pretended the evening hadn't happened, and we ignored each other again.

During Christmas 1969, Richard asked me if I wanted to go to a New Year's celebration with him. Of course, I wanted to—I wanted nothing more. The problem was, one day earlier, a boy from the Jewish Community had invited me to his New Year's party. My father had immediately consented, but I didn't want to go. I wanted to go with Richard. For days, I wondered if I should somehow talk to my father again—but how I would even do that now about a German boy?—or if I should just secretly go with Richard. I was in such anguish about it that I finally explained my dilemma to my mother. Together we talked to my father and to my greatest surprise, he relented. "Yes, then go, already."

I was elated, in shock over how my dad had agreed I could go. But I was also upset because it had all taken too long. At that point, it was already almost 4:00 p.m. on New Year's Eve. I dove into the bathroom, quickly combed my hair, applied lipstick and slipped into my favorite mini dress. Damn it, damn it, damn it, I thought to myself as I hastily packed my purse. I had no idea where Richard was. Since I had never replied, he couldn't know that I wanted to attend the party with him. I didn't know his phone number. I persuaded my mother to drive me to Richard's home. He had told me once where he lived. Mom, my staunch supporter, brought me there and waited in the car for me. I ran to Richard's apartment and his mother opened the door.

"Hello, I am Elke, a friend of Richard's," I said, out of breath, to the completely surprised lady. "Do you know where he is?"

"Oh, Richard already went to a party just a little while ago. I am not even sure exactly where." She noticed how distraught I was and tried to cheer me up. "I believe I am also not going to see him until next year." She laughed.

I said goodbye, shakily went down the stairs, and walked as if in a trance to my mother waiting in the car. There I collapsed on the seat. Richard was somewhere at a party having fun—without me—just because I didn't know if I could go with him in time. I was devastated, this was all too much. We drove home. Something in me was shifting. I was no longer sad or furious, just tired of fighting my dad. It was all too much work and would not be satisfying anyhow. I knew it would never be simple and just a straightforward courtship. A relationship with Richard was not going to be, and I might as well give up.

At home, I pulled myself together and waited for Daniel, the young man from the Jewish community to pick me up. From now on, as of midnight, I was not going to put myself in those difficult situations. I could only stare into the future concentrating on what came a step at a time.

First of all, I concentrated on school. I finished my apprenticeship and received an award from the government of Bavaria. Finally, I was able to go to school every day, one year at the secondary school, to receive my graduation diploma. I loved every subject; it didn't matter if it was math, chemistry or physics. In the cafeteria before school started, it made me proud when the boys asked me what answers I came up with on my homework. I also enjoyed my role as class representative, even though I occasionally had doubts about whether I was really able to do it.

On the day the graduation diplomas were handed out, I gave a speech to all the graduates and their relatives. I was terribly nervous, but many people told me how much they liked what I had to say.

What made me even happier that day was when my father gave me a bouquet of flowers, a dozen gorgeous roses. I am not sure if he had selected them as carefully as the roses for Hanna, but am convinced that day meant a lot to him, even though I hadn't necessarily done what he wanted. His facial paralysis was hardly recognizable anymore, and it made me happy to see him as he used to be.

The same evening, after they had awarded the diplomas, my father revealed the plans he was thinking of for me. I would work in a tax office. My father knew many people in Straubing, and among them was, of course, someone who owned such an office. This is where I would begin as an apprentice. After all, businesses would always need a good tax consultant. This made sense to me.

Two years later, I had also finished that vocational training, with an excellent reference from the tax consultant. Everyone now expected me to keep on working in the office. As much as I enjoyed being there, and as much as I respected the tax consultant, I just couldn't stay. Daniel, the young man from the Jewish community whom I had been with since that memorable New Year's Eve in 1969 was going to study pharmacy in Munich. And I decided to go with him. It was my chance to get away from the store and to get out of Straubing. It had always been my dream to live in a big city. My father was against this, of course, so Daniel and I got engaged.

I liked and appreciated my fiancé a lot. He was kind and paid loving attention to me. He was funny and smart. We enjoyed each other's company, had fun going out with friends, skiing, and loved going dancing at least once a week. In Munich we set up a small apartment in Schwabing, a popular district for students in the heart of the city.

On the surface my life was ticking along just fine. I had a secure existence, nothing too complicated to handle. But it didn't take long before I could tell that my work in the tax office was not meaningful to me. Instead of agonizing over the charts and rules, I was much more interested in the personal stories of the clients. Often, people who had come to the office for tax advice opened up to me and talked about their failed relationships or problems with their children or their parents. I loved listening. Instead of studying complicated books on tax law in the evening, I acquired books about psychology, which I read late into the night. I realized that working in the tax office was so different from who I really was. I asked myself what my purpose was in this world and what I should really be doing. Would it be possible to find out more about what would fulfill me?

After a workday of preparing balance sheets and profit and loss statements, I met up with a good friend. He was studying social work in Munich and was enthusiastic about his subjects, the internships and the other students. "Do you really believe that someone like you would be happy in a butcher's shop or a tax office, Elke?" he asked, stating the obvious.

He made a good point. It was time for me to change something.

From then on, I wanted only one thing, to study social work and work with people instead of numbers and tables.

But how could this happen? I was convinced I would have no chance at a school for social work. What I had was a completed apprenticeship as a saleswoman and experience as a tax consultant—how was this connected to social work? I had many doubts.

I spoke of this to my friend. He empathized with my dilemma and suggested that he ask the director of his college. "Maybe they will make an exception," he said, grinning at me. I was grateful he would try but did not have much hope. It was inconceivable to me that a social work college with a completely different professional focus would take someone like me. I thought it was most likely that when they looked at my history, they would think I just didn't know what I wanted.

But I knew exactly what I wanted. I had just buried it for too long. Two days later I met with my friend after work again. He had good news. "I have spoken with the director. He agreed you should come and introduce yourself. Just make an appointment with the secretary."

I was speechless—maybe it was possible! I immediately called the school the next morning and a day later was on my way to meet with the director.

On the ride to the city college, I watched the other people in the subway, wondering if they were going to the exact job they had been trained in, or whether some would rather be doing something else. I was excited. Now I had the opportunity to turn everything around and do what I really wanted to do. Half an hour before the agreed-upon time I was already at the school. I did not want to arrive late and make a bad first impression.

I sat impatiently in front of the director's office, watching the other students. They seemed relaxed and happy—a bit like I imagined the hippies in San Francisco to be. Here, no one wore a suit and analyzed tables and forms with a stern eye. I felt comfortable.

The door opened and an older man came out. “Fräulein Michalowicz?” he asked me, smiling.

“Yes, that’s me,” I stammered. My hands were embarrassingly damp with excitement. We shook hands and went into his office.

I put all the documents I had brought with me on his desk: my diplomas from Straubing and the recommendation of the Straubinger tax consultant. As he picked up each sheet and read it through, I told him I knew how difficult it most likely would be to change my field of study and switch to social work. At first, he said nothing. He looked at me again and again and read a few more lines. Was this a good sign? I had no idea. Then he put my documents to one side. “So, these are really very excellent report cards, Fräulein Michalowicz.” He leaned back in his chair and smiled at me, “Don’t worry, my dear. If we could not make an exception for someone like you, we would not be a good school. I like to choose my students myself, and for someone like you, with your achievements, I would be happy to make an exception.”

I was so excited, I could hardly believe what I just heard. My dream was actually within the realm of possibility. I would study social work!

But the next moment I remembered another challenge—since I hadn’t thought I would be accepted I had avoided thinking about it.

“Oh, thank you. I really appreciate it—I really want to go to this school,” I said. “But I have to talk to my father, now. He would have to support me financially.”

"Of course, no problem. Just contact me when you know more."

We said goodbye. I couldn't be completely happy. If I were to study here, it would mean being dependent on my parents again.

On Friday night I took the train to Straubing to see my parents. My father was sitting in his living room, watching TV. I wanted to settle things quickly and began immediately. "Dad, you know a friend of mine is studying social work in Munich?"

"Yes, I know," he answered, and continued staring at the TV. "I also know that his parents are not exactly happy about it."

I knew his parents were often in the shop. Great, I thought, this is going well.

I know now that he did not want to put down my professional aspirations—he wanted his daughter to be taken care of and he could not see beyond the terror of an uncertain future. For me, however, it became clearer every day. I would have to fight through the anxiety uncertainty brings, and just maybe the result would be worth the fight. "You know, he is really enjoying his studies and recently he said it would suit me, too."

My father switched to another channel and continued to ignore me.

"That's why," I said timidly, "that is why I met the director of the school last week. It isn't easy for me, with my educational background from another field, to get in." I cleared my throat. "Do you know what's the most amazing thing?" I tried to speak louder, "They would be willing to take me!"

Again I felt the pride and the joy I had felt earlier when talking to the director. My father had to be happy about that.

Slowly he turned his head and looked at me sternly.

"What exactly are you talking about?" he hissed.

"Dad, it's what I want to do. I want to help other people. You would just have to support me for a few years until I'm finished. I promise I'll work hard and have a permanent job again soon." I tried to smile, though I sensed the mood had gone downhill.

"What do you think your career would be? What could you do with a degree like that? Breaking up stones while you starve like I did in Mauthausen? It's going to come to that. You will not get a good job studying social work. With that kind of degree, you may not have any job, you may just work in a stone quarry," he shouted.

He jumped up; his face turned red. He was not finished yet. "You're throwing away everything, everything you have achieved until now! Can't you see?" He gasped for air. "Over my dead body! I'll never let you. I forbid you to go to that school. No good will come out of it!"

I had two choices: I could give up meekly or do the complete opposite of what he wanted. I would have to forget about studying social work in Munich. I would never be able to afford it.

I just stood there, trying not to cry, and said calmly, "Good. If that's the way it is, I know that it's possible to study psychology in Toronto. From Sollie I know students are able to work while studying there and I would not have to rely on anyone. I will do exactly that. I don't need your help."

With those final words, I turned around, ran out of the living room and slammed the door behind me. There would be no more appeasing, no more silence, only fury to motivate me to do what I was meant to do. I was of the same ilk as my dad. You push me too far and I fight tooth and nail for what I think is right. Ironically that trait came straight from him. If he could survive having everything taken from him and start all over from scratch at twenty, so could I.

The die was cast. I had made my decision to give up my job, my fiancé and my family to go to Canada to study. Not social work, but psychology was the direction I wanted to go. My father had struggled hard to be settled and secure for the last twenty years and now I was bringing risk into his life again. He could only see the difficulties and uncertainty I was facing. I understand now through my experience as a therapist that his traumatic memories would have been triggered with my wanting to delve into some vague study of the human mind.

In his case it meant exploring inner recesses that he was trying to forget, the anguish, pain and anger that only burst through once in a while in a crisis, but mostly could be contained. In post-trauma life, the mind attaches itself to anything familiar. My wanting to delve into the areas of damage was like me wanting to cut open his head and trying to make sense of the chaos that was nestled inside. How could that ever be accomplished? How could that ever be successful? The doctor in Munich certainly couldn't help, and Alex himself figured out that focusing on work was a successful memory suppressant. Of course his creating safety around himself had become very self-reinforcing. He could not venture too far from the new life as usual anymore. I did not know if I'd be successful, but I did know that I had to challenge those very restrictive boundaries.

I know now that he did not want to put down my professional aspirations—he wanted his daughter to be taken care of and he could not see beyond the terror of an uncertain future. For me, however, it became clearer every day. I would have to fight through the anxiety uncertainty brings, and just maybe the result would be worth the fight.

Although I prepared as well as I could, made inquiries about academic study in Canada and had a long talk with Sollie on the phone, I really did not know what to expect there. I often asked myself if I'd be able to pull it off. Sometimes I wondered if I was crazy or daring to think I could do it—but which one was it?

On my way back to Munich on the train after my visit to Straubing, I thought about what it was like when I had visited Canada for the first time at eighteen with Daniel, my fiancé. He had relatives in New York whom we visited, and it had been sticky and scorching hot there. Smoky air came out of sewer covers and yellow taxis idled in traffic jams in Times Square.

In the shops, I almost froze to death. Air-conditioning blasted ice-cold from every corner of the room. I only had mini dresses, all the rage in 1972, and I had goose bumps and felt chilled the whole time.

The next few days we stayed in south Manhattan and visited the Guggenheim Museum. When we left New York, I remembered the city as never-ending communities of vibrant, flashy and opinionated people. It was fun and stimulating, but not relaxing.

Toronto, on the other hand, was more of the latter. People were more casual and open; the city, calmer. I wanted to see the campus of the University of Toronto, which my cousin Sollie had recommended. We sat on the lawn in front of the main building, with its mighty stone towers and impressive arched windows. The university was almost like a castle to me, and in this castle were young people who did exactly what I wanted to do: study psychology. The campus was like a small city, a world of its own. I was fascinated.

After Toronto, we had traveled to Montreal, to my Aunt Hanna. This was the visit I had longed for since that day in Munich on Leopold Street. I wanted to see how my family lived there. They had a house in the Côte-Saint-Luc area, a very nice English-speaking area. When I stood with my fiancé in front of Hanna's door, I could hardly breathe, I was so excited.

Finally, I had done it. My Canadian family had received me as warmly as they had at the airport in Munich when I first met them. What struck me immediately was that my aunt made a great effort at keeping the house spotless. Everything was in pale shades and everywhere she had placed boxes of Kleenex tissues. I was not used to this at home, where I had always been trained to use paper as sparingly as possible. But here in my aunt's house, the rules were different. Aunt Hanna was an excellent cook. Every day she prepared Yiddish food from scratch: delicious meatballs, latkes, and chicken soup.

One day at breakfast, she suggested making lokshen, handmade noodles my dad had loved at home. Several hours alone in the kitchen with my aunt was like a dream come true for me.

As we rolled out the dough, she inquired, "Elke, would you like to know a bit more about what I found out about our father and your grandfather, Arye?" I nodded. Her wanting to share with me was special. She told me Arye tried to fight to the bitter end in an effort to protect his family and not leave a stone unturned to get them back. But instead he was killed instantly and my grandparents' house now belonged to the communists in Poland, where they built a school. "We don't have any rights to it," she said, sighing. She continued kneading the dough. "But besides your grandfather being murdered so senselessly, do you know what the worst thing is?"

I shrugged my shoulders and shook my head.

"The farmer who betrayed my father was just handed a piece of our property. He is just a parasite, not a man. And they were all complicit, not admitting that responsibility in someone's hands might exist!" Her eyes filled with tears and her hands began to tremble. She clutched the rolling pin tight in her hand while pulling up her sleeve with the other. "But I can only hope there is a reckoning," her voice grew louder again. "How can anyone live with themselves acting so despicably? There is no redemption for that! In the end Alex and I did survive and Hitler is the one who is dead. Hitler is the coward who committed suicide because he could not face the consequences for his actions."

I certainly understood her anger and shared her sense of outrage. I wished I could have done more. Instead I told her I was amazed at how much she found out and complimented her on the research she did over many years. I was sorry my Aunt Hanna was shut down in her effort to make sense of it all for herself. There were too many villains and no way to make sense of it. It's up to each person to hold themselves accountable, to make the world a better place, I thought to myself, and maybe this is where I first thought the story of my family needed to be told.

I had a few hours to reminisce about all this during the train ride from Straubing to Munich. I had promised my Aunt Hanna to come back to Canada at some point. Would I be able to actually make this happen and pick up where we left off? My dad never could take the journey, though he tried for years. Maybe it would be me who could actually do it. Maybe this was the life I was meant to live, in Canada. People had been so open and welcoming, and I wanted to see who I would be among them. The English language intrigued me—the casual way of speaking and how words rolled off English speakers' tongues so smoothly. German felt too exacting and guttural in comparison. The thought of becoming a fluent English speaker was very appealing.

The next morning, I was sitting at my desk in the tax office again, working on a spreadsheet. I secretly stretched my feet under the table and slipped out of my ballet flats. I imagined feeling sand with my toes and wading into the ocean. To admire the blue ocean, to feel the sun and no longer sit under these neon tubes. I knew without a shadow of a doubt I was not going to spend my life at this desk.

In those days, when I was deciding my future and if I was going to go to Canada, I also realized I did not want to marry my fiancé. This decision came gradually, but then suddenly there was no return. I just couldn't stay with him, even though I appreciated him deeply. This was not my future, not here and not with him.

That evening after work I told him what I had decided. It broke my heart to see him crying, just like I was. But what could I have done? I had to be honest with him. I had to leave. I had another life to live. At that point, I did not want to be someone's wife, to have children, to sit around the house and water the flowers in the garden.

I told him I had booked a trip to Greece that afternoon, alone, and that I would never have told him if I hadn't been sure.

Of course, I was still scared and wavered back and forth, doubting that I could and would actually do it. I vowed that if I still wanted to leave after the Greece trip, I would do it as quickly as possible, no matter how much resistance I received or how difficult it would be.

The night after the conversation with my fiancé was terrible. Of course, I felt guilty, but I would not have been able to stay in our apartment—which I'd once loved so much—for one second longer. Everything had become too narrow, too stuck, too predictable. I was twenty-one and I wanted to brave the world.

A week later I stood with my suitcase at the airport in Athens. I took a ferry to the island of Ios, between Naxos and Santorini. On the first afternoon, I explored the island. The grass covering the hills was withered and brown from the powerful sun. I loved the white houses, the blue dome roofs, the palm trees. The air smelled fresh and salty and I felt I could breathe again. I walked along the narrow paths between the old whitewashed houses down to the ocean. At the beach, I took off my ballerina flats and felt the grainy sand under my feet. For me, this meant freedom. It didn't bother me that the sand was hot from the sun. Gingerly, I walked to the water. There I stood, the ocean flowing over my feet, looking out over the brilliant turquoise Aegean Sea.

I was right to come here, I thought, putting my hands in the water. I had left all my worries and fears behind and had simply done what I wanted. It felt good. I watched the white sailboats; the sun warmed my skin. I went one step farther into the ocean and had the feeling that the world had opened itself before me. Looking out over the blue-green water, I could clearly see there was space for me to create who and how I wanted to be. I just needed to trust that I would figure it out—one step at a time. At that moment, I was sure as never before. I had the courage.

I was going to Canada.

On my travels in Europe

Here I am 19 and moving to Munich

PART THREE

Chapter 13

Cabbagetown and psychic dreams

Toronto and Vancouver, Canada, 1975–2004

I HAD A WINDOW SEAT ON THE PLANE AND WATCHED AS I left the European continent behind and flew over the Atlantic, away from my home. I was really doing it, how crazy was that? Unlike on my vacation to the United States and Canada a couple of years earlier, this time, no return flight was booked. While the other passengers slept or read books and newspapers, I could not stop looking out at where we were hovering somewhere in space. How far away were we from Straubing? How long would it be before we arrived in Toronto and my new life finally began? I leaned back into the seat. I felt the weeks of tension—the quarrel with my father, the separation from my fiancé, the farewell to my friends—slowly fading. The monotonous sound of the air conditioning did its best to calm me.

During the hours over the ocean, I tried to come to terms with what was happening, to clear my head. Was my cousin Sollie shocked that I was actually on my way to Toronto? At that thought I had to smile. I don't think he expected that. But he was the one who initially gave me the idea through his tales of studying in Canada. Strictly speaking, it was his own fault I would soon be standing at his door.

Later, I pressed my face to the window and recognized the shape of the land on the horizon. It would not be long before I was there, the place that had intrigued me since my family visited from Canada.

At that moment, I remembered Jacob, as he had stood arm in arm with my father on Leopold Street. How he had told my father about Hanna and Canada. It felt as if it were yesterday. That one encounter had created a seismic shift in my life. The appearance of my Canadian family had unleashed a series of events that shifted the world as I knew it and all the people I loved with it. And now, ten years later, I was at the airport in Toronto at the baggage claim, waiting for my suitcase.

Sollie was already waiting for me. He grinned and hugged me. The first thing I told him was that I would not get on his nerves and would find a place to live as fast as I could. He just smiled and helped me with my luggage. I considered myself lucky he was in Toronto a couple of months at just at the right time, before he returned to Montreal to continue his master's degree. The next morning I bought a newspaper, and I was encouraged that my English was sufficient to read all the rental offers. Finding an apartment for less than one hundred dollars a month seemed hopeless though. "Look for shared accommodation. You'll get something cheap for sure," Sollie advised.

A few days later I was ringing a doorbell. While I waited and hoped someone would answer, I marveled at the house. It reminded me of one of the little houses in the book of the Brothers Grimm, which I had always read with my grandfather. A mixture of the house of the Seven Dwarfs, with tiny pewter glass windows, and the gingerbread house from Hansel and Gretel. Someone pressed the door handle down from the inside and the dark green door opened with a creak. In front of me stood a young man who smiled and said in heavily accented German, "You must be Elke, right?" I had talked to him the day before.

He was the landlord and had been born in Germany, but he had lived in Canada all his life. He rented a floor in the house to two Canadian girls. He showed me my room with a red carpeted floor and bright white walls—after all the flats I had viewed, I was happy to see that the house was very clean and there was not a single mark on the carpet. It smelled fresh, the two girls were nice, and I immediately felt comfortable. When he told me the rent would cost only ninety dollars, I could have hugged him. That same evening, Sollie drove me back with my suitcases.

The place was in an area of Toronto called Cabbagetown. I was relieved not to be a burden to Sollie, and I was quite proud to have found a place so quickly. Now I did not want to waste time and wanted to look around my new neighborhood. I had already fallen in love with the Victorian houses with the red tile bricks on the drive over.

I slipped into my little furry jacket, zipped up my long leather boots and marched off. People were safely settled behind softly lit bay windows in their brick houses. It was very quiet, and I found the area a bit deserted, but it had sometimes been like that on Schlesische Street. I continued on and decided to go to the main street. Maybe I would meet a few people, out on a crisp night.

The main street certainly was busy. There were lots of men, who seemed to be the ones wandering about in the evening. Many stared at me and some of them came up to me and muttered something. I chastised myself for not understanding them. I had thought my school English would be enough to understand the basics, but what were they talking about? Some smelled of alcohol, but I did not want to be impolite. Suddenly, it occurred to me I could use the phrase Sollie had taught me a couple of days ago. I was supposed to say, "Pardon me?" and then people would know I did not understand, and they would repeat it. Carefully, I enunciated, "Pardon me?" The men looked at me blankly, some shook their heads and eventually walked away. When one of them asked "Hey, babe, how much?" the penny finally dropped. Something was terribly wrong, I shuddered, realizing the kind of place this was. I knew areas like this existed in big cities, but had never actually seen one, let alone walked around in them. This was a **bad** idea to come here. I had to get out of here. As quickly as possible, I turned and hurried back to the fairytale house with the nice roommates.

I ran the whole way back, thinking I could hear one of those men following me. I trembled as I searched for the key and hurriedly opened the door. I slammed it behind me and pushed the latch shut.

"Where were you just now?" one of the two girls asked me a few minutes later when we met in the shared kitchen. I had already calmed down; after all, nothing had happened. "Oh, just a walk, a little look around," I replied. My roommate stared at me with her mouth open. Then she shouted, "Do not ever walk around in the dark! Absolutely not ever! This is not a safe place at night! During the day is different, you can go out then." She flapped her hands wildly in case I didn't understand the meaning.

Wo bin ich gelandet? I asked myself. What kind of place have I ended up in? But my English conversational skills weren't enough to discuss this in any meaningful way with my new roommates.

I bid them good night, went to my room and lay down on my bed. I was no longer in Straubing. I had to be aware. I had to learn how fast things could change here, from day to night, from street to street, from house to house. Since she had said it was okay to walk around in the daytime, I got up the next morning ready to brave it all. I did not wear a mini dress as I had the night before but put on my long coat, determined to explore the area.

During the day, as usual, everything looked quite different. People were on their way to work, getting into buses or red-and-white streetcars; elderly people walked to buy a newspaper. There was no trace of the strange atmosphere of last night. I strolled through the streets, looking at every house, every street sign, every display in the shop windows. The air was pure and cool. The cold here—dry and icy—was different from that in Straubing. The sun shone and there wasn't a whiff of Danube fog in the air.

Then I smelled it, the scent of freshly baked bread. I was standing right in front of the shop window of a bakery. Of course, I thought about my parents' shop, and I had to go inside. The glass counter was almost as long as the one in our store. Behind it were lemon tarts, cinnamon rolls and apple swirls rather than white sausages and ham. A young woman, probably an apprentice, was just filling a shelf. She reminded me of my time as a trainee in my parents' shop.

This was my first shopping experience in Canada on my own. While I was here visiting my family on vacation a couple of years before I had never gone shopping without them.

Behind the counter stood an older woman who smiled at me and asked, “Hello, dear. How are you today?”

I was startled. Was she talking to me? She did not even know me. I understood the words, but why did she want to know how I was? I was suspicious. In Germany when you inquire how somebody is doing you know them very well and you are really interested in their wellbeing. Why would she be interested in me? But the woman continued to smile, even though I looked at her with shock. I looked around, but since I was the only one in the store, I ordered two buns.

I did not know how to assess what she’d just said to me. Again, I thought of my father and heard him say, “Elke, there are always good and bad people. You have to figure it out—and do not let yourself be taken in. This woman looked like she had very good intentions. I grinned back shyly, took my two buns, nodded, whispered goodbye and left the store.

Within a few days, I realized that in Toronto, this was a standard welcome and most people added a “How are you?” to their “Hello.” Except for, “Well, thanks, and you?” they didn’t really want to hear anything else.

That was precisely why I had to agree with Gerhard, my German landlord, who advised me to learn more English. The first thing he said was that we would not speak German to each other, even when we were alone together. “A big part of learning English is to immerse yourself totally in it. Read some simple books and never mind if you don’t understand everything. Just keep going till you get the meaning of the overall story,” he said, handing me my first little English book, called *Eric*.

About three weeks after my arrival I visited some of Gerhard's English-speaking friends with him, in a lake town in Ontario. They spoke over top of each other and the conversation was very fast. As the three of them laughed and chatted, I sat next to them, feeling excluded. I had thought my English was much better than it was, and the school English I'd learned seemed useless for university. My mind kept spinning. How would I manage to even apply for university, let alone sit in a lecture and understand what the professor was talking about? I could not even understand three different people talking about nothing of importance! I spoke to Gerhard about it on our drive back to Toronto.

He suggested I enroll in an English as a Second Language class at a community college and inspired me to practice for an English test called the TOEFL. This Test of English as a Foreign Language had reading, listening, speaking and writing sections and was four hours long. Gerhard happened to be an ESL teacher and was very knowledgeable about the requirements. He was another one of those uncanny circumstances, an angel along the way, for which I have been infinitely grateful throughout my life. Gerhard told me I would be able to write this test more than once and encouraged me to give it a try as soon as possible to see how much it I could do. He was right. The first time I got slightly under the percentage I needed to get into university. I was most worried about the writing part and the score requirement would be a challenge for most native English speakers. But the second time, three months after I arrived in Canada, I passed with a higher than required score and completed an important prerequisite to get into university.

The girl who had stood behind the counter of her parents' deli a few years earlier was ready to fill out a lengthy and complicated university admission form. A few months later, her outlandish wish came true when she opened the letter stating that Elke Maria Michalowicz was accepted into the Bachelor of Arts program at the University of Toronto.

The only contact I had with my parents at this time was letters, as phoning was too inconvenient because of the time change and too expensive. I was trying to stick to a budget of three hundred dollars a month, including rent, so I could stretch the cash my mom had secretly given me as long as possible. She was still my staunch supporter, though without a doubt, both of them must have felt very abandoned by me. Since the fighting spirit that had erupted between Dad and me, what would have happened had he said, "No, you will do no such thing. I am not going to lose you too!" Only just come of age at twenty-one, still quite vulnerable and empathetic under all my bravado, would I have surrendered? Instead, he just let me go.

There was a clear incongruence between his words not supporting my psychology aspirations and his actions. Maybe this was the real act of love of both of my parents—to let me go. No stranger to fortitude, to muster all their strength and keep going, they kicked into that mode yet again. Now they stood without me in the shop, which they had built from nothing. Who would take it over now? They would not have expected their only daughter to leave them alone. Had the existence of my extended Canadian family not brought on the seismic shift in our lives, I would surely not have dreamed of the journey away from my home.

Now I had been in Canada just a few short months and I was ready for university. I would make both my parents proud. I told myself I had to be right about that and not fail.

I carefully read the course descriptions, because I wanted to avoid having to write homework and essays in English. I was just not confident enough in the language. There was an endless amount of vocabulary that I did not know. Even if I understood the meaning of a sentence, I had to look up some words to understand the meaning of the whole story. So, I started with courses that had exams in multiple-choice format. For every book or essay I had to read for the course, I needed at least three times longer than for a German text. In the evenings, I sat on my bed and went over every line.

My attention had to be impeccable. If my concentration slipped for only a second and I accidentally read the next line, it would not make any sense. Then I had to go back and start over. I forced myself to look up every word I did not know. Every careless mistake I made I would pay for with additional study time later.

When we learned of the date of the first psychology exam, I marked the day in my calendar. Several weeks earlier I began to study for it every night, until my eyes fell shut long after midnight. The next day, when the alarm clock rang, I would wake up amid books, papers and pencils. After the first few days my neck ached—if you concentrate on every word as I had to do, you sit differently and the body tenses. When I closed my eyes, the letters danced in front of me, I was straining so hard. But I did not give up. I opened them again and read the sentence one more time.

During the exam I was very nervous, but I made a huge effort to focus on understanding the meaning of the questions and not make careless mistakes that I would bitterly regret later. I felt like I was at school again when Sister Michaela had encouraged me. When I handed in the exams, I thought to myself that I was sure I'd passed the test. That changed, however, when I heard the others talking. I was unsure. They were all first-language English speakers. What if I had misunderstood some questions? What if I did not understand what the professor wanted? I felt faint. Did I really think I would be able to handle an exam right away, just like them? The others were arguing about their answers.

A week later we got the results. Now I was even more nervous—now I would learn the truth. I held the paper with my name on it in my hand. I was trembling. Where was the grade? I only knew the German system of grades: 1 (very good) to 6 (insufficient). On these exams, however, the professor had scribbled percentages that I could not even read properly. Finally, I turned to my neighbor in the lecture hall. "What do these numbers mean? Can you help me?" She looked at my exam. "Oh, wow!" she said, smiling. "That means 97 percent! You have 97 percent out of 100! That's really good." She showed me her test, and the number was smeared there too. "Look, I've got 70 percent. I'm really proud of that. But 97 percent is something else ..."

For me, the outcome was not just a good grade. I finally had the confirmation that I was on the right track. That course seemed to suit me. Having better grades than most of the first-language speakers gave me confidence. Maybe I do have a natural understanding of this and a knack for psychology, I thought.

My spoken English was definitely getting better too, and I even started dreaming in it. I had easy exchanges with the women at the supermarket checkout and chatted with other students in the lecture hall. Yet the most interesting thing I had learned so far in the course was that I had natural empathy: the ability to put yourself into other people's shoes. That was a given in my family, and I started to get an appreciation of this strength being the foundation for my parents' morals and successes. Coupled with their immense fortitude to keep going during tough times, they had inadvertently equipped me to stick to the university program. There was no backing out now.

In my second year of university I had to take a course on German literature from the nineteenth century. Two professors offered this course, and one was German, so I thought I should take the course with him. But I already had a bad feeling in the first lecture.

I didn't like him. His movements, the way he appraised his students, looking down his nose at them, how his eyes flashed—all of it bothered me. I did not feel comfortable in his course. Then I remembered my father again. What would he have done? But there was a problem. Almost all the students wanted to be with the German professor. The lectures were almost overcrowded because the other professor's course was considered much too difficult.

That professor had studied German literature in Oxford and spoke with an upper-class English accent that hardly anyone understood. When I told a few others that I was thinking about switching classes, they looked at me in shock. "What? He only gives bad grades. You will never make it. You will mess up your whole grade point average—no one has ever gotten a very good mark from him." But I already knew that I had no choice. I had to get out of the course with the German professor.

The next week I went to the Oxford professor's lecture. Only five people were sitting in the room. When he came in, I realized what the others had meant. He stared ahead, deeply absorbed in thought, his lips pressed tightly against each other. He wore an old tweed suit, and his horn-rimmed glasses were from an era long past. I had the impression he had fallen behind the times, but as he began to talk, I felt his enthusiasm and devotion for what he was doing. Even then I knew that my decision had been the right one. Now I just had to understand him …

I wrote down every word he said as fast as I could. That meant many more long nights at home, translating his sentences first to understand them. I always had what the other students said about him in the back of my mind: that nobody had ever received a really good grade from him. But I did not let that scare me. I was impressed with what he knew, and I was simply trying to understand what he was saying.

In the middle of the semester we had to hand in our first assignment: researching something in the library and writing an essay of at least twenty pages. You could choose the topic and I chose Heinrich Heine. I did not have the slightest idea how to write such essays—so far, I had managed to complete only courses with multiple-choice questions. After a long day at the library and many hours of research at my desk, I decided to not to worry about all the various opinions and write what I thought about Heine. Then I added a few opinions from literature specialists to complete the picture. I did not have high hopes that I would pass the course with a good grade, but so be it. It took a few weeks before he marked all the essays.

One morning he came into the lecture hall with his worn-out brown leather bag, unlocked it and pulled out the articles. There they were, and somewhere in the stack was my assignment. He called up each of the five students who had ventured into his course, in alphabetical order. My neighbor had a "C+" on her assignment. She told me that in Canada, besides the percentage marks, there were also letter grades for essays. "A" was excellent, "F" was failure. In all the excitement, I had not noticed that the professor had not called my name yet. He was already at the end of the alphabet.

He cleared his throat and pushed his large glasses further back on his nose. "There is an assignment that I would now like to speak about in greater detail, Elke's essay on Heine." He looked at me. I was hot and cold at the same time. I just nodded. Damn, I thought to myself, I should have stayed within the guidelines and not written my own interpretations. "Because, Elke," he continued, "I've marked your work A+."

The others whispered and turned to look at me.

I was happy I had not given too much credence to what the other students said about this lecturer. He was a fine man, smart and sincere. Just like Sister Michaela in Grade Two, he also clearly valued my perceptions. This professor suggested I might want to pursue an academic career in German literature and become a professor myself. He promised to give me references should I need them. I felt like I had in the bakery on my first solo shopping excursion. Was he talking to me? Since there was nobody else around, I came to the conclusion he must be, but he really didn't understand how out of my depth I was in his course. I could not blame him. After all, he had no idea that I was just an imposter in his class, that I was just the girl who stood behind the counter at my parents' store a few years earlier.

I struggled with this total lack of confidence for the first few years of university. But each time I was flooded with feelings of not being good enough, I brought back the memory of that professor's confidence in me. There must be something to it then, I had to admit—both he and Sister Michaela couldn't have been totally out to lunch.

There were times when I was debating if a career as a German professor would suit me, but it was my knack for empathy and the desire to work with people like my dad who wanted to overcome psychological trauma that won out, hands down.

I graduated with distinction from the University of Toronto with a Bachelor of Psychology and a minor in German literature. Nobody was prouder than my parents when I sent them a photo with the bachelor gown over my shoulders and the obligatory hat with tassel on my head.

We wrote frequent letters to each other and my parents loved getting the annual photo albums I made for them for each year of my life in Canada. I also visited them, usually for a few weeks during the summer. My parents' conversations with customers had shifted dramatically. Now enthusiastic exclamations like "Oh, our Elke, she is well on her way to becoming a psychologist in Canada" were the new norm. They had embraced my life in Toronto.

I too had moved and now lived with a few roommates in an old Victorian house on Markham Street. I had a committed boyfriend who I loved very much. He was sensitive, emotional and incredibly talented, spoke seven languages, played viola and performed as an actor in theater. He was a special person who once memorized a German monologue for a play phonetically without knowing a word of German. Each morning he ran fifteen kilometers and then he cycled with me through Toronto. He was from an intellectual, wealthy Toronto family that had encouraged him to do a master's program in history at Oxford. Now that he was back in Toronto, he wondered which direction to take; history, languages or art. One day, after we had talked through all his options, I bid him goodbye for the afternoon and got on my bike to cycle to the Clarke Institute, an important psychiatric facility in Toronto, where I volunteered one afternoon a week.

As I cycled down the street away from our house, a German shepherd growled at me. I had already seen it out of the corner of my eye and had started thinking of my father and his beloved dogs. But this dog seemed to have it out for me. It started to run after me, and I heard its panting. I pedaled as fast as I possibly could. It is going to bite my leg, I thought. As I struggled, slipping off the pedals at least three times, I turned my head back to see how close it was—only a few centimeters behind me, baring its teeth and barking. I screamed and suddenly heard a loud bang. I crashed into a parked car and was flung, with my bike, over the side of the car to land on the sidewalk. Dammit! I thought to myself as the right side of my body landed hard on the pavement.

A woman came running. "For God's sake! Are you still alive? Can you hear me? Hello? For God's sake!" She looked at me, frightened. "That bloody beast!" She was completely beside herself. Then I suddenly remembered. Where was the dog? Would he bite me in the leg, now that I was so helpless? I jerked and tried to sit up. But he was nowhere to be seen. Slowly I stood up, knees wobbly. "I'm okay," I murmured, my lips trembling.

"You have to go to the hospital," the woman said, grabbing my arm as if to support me.

"What? No, I have to go to work now. I am already late."

"No, you don't! You are in shock. You must go to the hospital. Can someone take you there?"

She asked me my name and repeated the sentence about the hospital at least three times. I lifted up my bike and saw that the front tire rim was bent and the inner tube had lost air. I would not be going anywhere with it like that.

I left the woman behind and pushed the bike home. I felt dazed, and with every step I felt my body aching. I also had some abrasions and painful bleeding. I was lucky. My boyfriend was at home and I saw by his expression how awful I must have looked. He persuaded me to go to the emergency room of a hospital. The doctor there told me I had been lucky. Nothing was broken and I had no internal injuries or concussion, just a black eye and bruises down my whole right side.

The spooky thing about this accident was what I dreamed afterwards. Still in shock, I told my boyfriend to come with me to bring my bicycle, which was so important to me, to a workshop. The man in the store, who skeptically inspected my bent wheel, frowned and said that it would cost at least seventy dollars. It was a huge sum for a student like me. But what could I do? I asked him to fix the bike and my boyfriend and I went home.

The cost preoccupied my thoughts and I wondered where I could save money. The night before I picked up the bike again, I had a dream: I was back in the bike shop, the cash register sounded a *ding* and I was told, "That will be thirty-four dollars and thirty-eight cents." I woke up and was relieved—the repair cost only half as much! Then I realized I had been dreaming and was disappointed.

I told my boyfriend about it and he laughed. "If this is true and he asks for exactly that amount today, you must immediately give everything up and become a fortune teller. I can see you in a lilac dress with a black cat on your shoulder in front of a glass ball." This image amused me too, and I laughed. He went back to running and I went to the garage. Behind the counter, the wife of the shopkeeper was just writing something on a pad of paper. I told her my name and described my bike to her. "Oh," she said cheerfully and nodded, "How do you want to pay? That will be thirty-four dollars and thirty-eight cents."

I wanted to pinch myself. What was going on? I was no longer in my dream. "Huh? I thought the repair was going to cost around seventy dollars. That's what your husband told me." I stared at her with my mouth open.

"You can still pay more if you absolutely want to," she said, laughing.

"No, no," I stammered, trying not to show her how mystified I was. When I pushed my bike out of the shop and the door closed behind me with a loud squeal, I said to myself, "If you ever doubt that there is more out there than the things we learn in a school textbook, then you must think of the thirty-four dollars and thirty-eight cents."

Even while completing my final papers towards a bachelor's degree, I made the decision to work before continuing with a master's degree. After the first replies to my work applications, however, I realized that with a bachelor's degree I would only be able to work in hospitals that treated drug addicts or with violent people. One offer I considered was working in a juvenile school for young men. But when I was told in the interview how I was supposed to handle someone coming at me with a knife, I made the decision to have a second look through the other responses.

My first official job was in a group home for girls. They had to leave their families because their parents could no longer take care of them or because the girls were violent, drug-dependent or had been expelled from school. I worked there for eighteen months, mostly in different shifts. Together with other social workers, I looked after five girls. During that time, I learned how to deal with seriously traumatized people. I often thought about my father, because those girls had experienced extreme physical and psychological violence and tried everything to repress the memories. And there were girls who passed on the violence.

Once I had to call the police as one of them went berserk and beat a roommate bloody. When I interfered and pulled her off, she threatened to kill me. Luckily, the director of the group home lived in a separate apartment upstairs. One of the other girls had banged on his door and he came rushing to my assistance just in time. A brawl ensued, like a scene in a bad Western movie. Except this one included a wiry fourteen-year-old girl with bloodshot eyes and a mighty punch. She swung at the director, who tried to pin her down, and she kicked him in the groin, then threatened his jugular with a broken Coke bottle. Luckily, the police arrived in time and the girl was transferred to a higher-security group home. The other girls in the group home were unpredictable too and after that incident I was worried about my own safety. But giving up was not an option. I needed to stay in this job to feel that I would not be intimidated and to show stability for my next job application.

My parents' fortitude had made mine pale by comparison. I would deal with the thugs, suck it up and get on with it. It was easy not to tell my parents about the dangers in this job, as they were so far away. I only related the good parts about my new career because they deserved to know I was doing well. But I was thinking those violent outbursts weren't sustainable in the long term. The kids were a difficult clientele, just like my dad had been difficult. There was too much trauma, violence and not a good prognosis for recovery. To work with an easier-to-deal-with, less traumatized adult group, I would have to return to university and complete a master's degree. Then I could find employment in a clinic or even be in private practice. I kept the job long enough to save some money and then quit.

I was very happy to be sitting in the auditorium on the first day of my master's. It was a soothing environment, in contrast to ensuring the mood in the group home was not spiraling into dangerous territory. I had decided on courses in adult education and counseling. Now I savored being able to read textbooks quietly in the library or write essays in my shared accommodations even more.

Because I had some money from my previous job, I was able to call my parents more often. One morning, while talking to my mother, I told her about my nice attic room. I described the beams, the sloping roof, the little windows looking out into the sky.

My mother fell silent. I did not know what was going on and continued to tell her about the furniture in the room and the window coverings that filtered the sun. She did not react.

Finally, she stammered, "Elke, I'm feeling a bit dizzy."

"Hey, Mom, what's going on?" I was worried. Was she dehydrated? Was she having circulatory problems?

"I never ended up telling you," she whispered, as if someone were listening.

"What? What have you never told me?" I feared the worst. My hands were trembling.

"Your great-grandmother Lucia, my grandmother, she had exactly the same kind of attic room ..." She told me that my great-grandmother in Straubing had been a fortune teller and had raised her five children during the First World War that way.

"I often played in it. I know exactly what it looked like," said my mother. "My God, Elke, it sounds as if it is exactly the same attic room!"

I got goosebumps and tears in my eyes. My mother in Straubing most likely felt the same way.

"Another thing I never told you," she whispered. "Lucia told me that I would have a daughter one day who would move across an ocean that will separate us. Now it has really happened."

After we hung up, I looked around my room. I had to laugh even as tears rolled down my cheeks. Maybe everything really was already "written."

The decision to take my master's degree also meant that my boyfriend and I had to part ways. He had accepted a job in foreign service and moved to Chile, and I could not imagine giving up everything for him. I had plans for myself. I had to complete my master's to be able to help people trapped in anxiety. My boyfriend's position would require moving from country to country—I wanted to stay in Canada and make a difference in people's lives. It was a calling, more than a career, and moving around was not an option for me. But I felt terribly vulnerable having lost a love I thought was going to last. I listened to Joni Mitchell croon about wishing for a river so she could skate away because she'd made her baby cry—while I cried my own river. What had I done? How could I let him go? Would I ever love somebody so wholeheartedly again?

In order to get a handle on this vulnerability, I added a practical course on gestalt therapy to my courses. *Gestalt* is a German word meaning "shape" or "form." Gestalt therapy was developed by Fritz Perls as an alternative to conventional Freudian analysis. It uses experiential techniques to enhance awareness, self-expression and self-direction.

The sessions were held by therapists who were on staff at the Gestalt Institute. The first year was group sessions in which we received our own therapy and we also had to fill a quota of individual sessions. Second-year students were co-leading workshops and group sessions, and third-year students also provided individual therapy sessions.

The well-defended fortress I had so carefully constructed was thoroughly torn down by the therapists and student trainees. There was nowhere to hide from those scary emotions I had buried somewhere deep inside. It turned out I was overflowing with inconsolable sadness and furious anger. It was very difficult for me. I struggled to be as honest with myself and actually allow myself to delve into those feelings. It felt dangerous, like I would never be able to stop feeling sad or angry, so deep was the pain. Ultimately, though, it was a relief to let those feelings out without restraint and not be judged for it.

Therapy is a joint venture. The group let me know that they could handle whatever I brought to the session and I grew more in connection with those people. Feeling the power of my anger actually helped strengthen my resolve to create a different life for myself. Paradoxically, feeling the depth of my parents' and my own pain helped me also to let it go.

This was a brilliant way of learning therapy, on oneself first, and I learned more than any theoretical model would teach me at university.

I learned a great deal about myself in Gestalt—about my childhood fears, the rage I felt and my abandonment issues. My biggest trauma was the loss of my grandfather whom I was very attached to. I had not securely attached to my parents over the first three years of my life, the most crucial time for this to happen.

Over time, I led workshops and private sessions myself and provided a safe haven for clients' emotional trauma. There is so much shame and darkness in people's hidden aspects, which are often hidden even from themselves. When they are able to put it out there, to be seen and received with compassion, it is very freeing. I became a master in providing this safe space but also in challenging people to move beyond the vulnerability, through their anger and ultimately make more empowered choices and live the life they wanted.

The highlight of the semester was when the founder and director of the Gestalt Institute of Scandinavia, John Porting, came to Toronto from Denmark as a guest lecturer for a weekend. He was my greatest role model and I was thrilled that he exemplified what I had felt was my strength as a therapist too. On one hand, he always made his clients feel they could trust him and feel safe with him. On the other, he challenged his clients and pushed them to work on their limitations and fundamentally change their lives.

After that weekend, John Porting spoke to me personally and told me in no uncertain terms that he thought I had a special gift. "You can be very empathetic and make people feel they can show you their innermost secrets. But you are tough, and you challenge them beyond their perceived limits." He smiled at me encouragingly. "I think you've got what it takes to co-lead this workshop I'm planning in Denmark." At his Gestalt Institute of Scandinavia, he was holding a three-week workshop for people from the clinical medical sector, such as doctors, nurses and social workers. "Wow, what is there to think about? You can count on me," I told him, grinning back.

On the plane to Denmark a month later, I again sat at the window and looked out. What a long road I had traveled already. Only a few years into my studies, and I was returning to Europe to help educate a group of social workers and medical professionals. Forget about me studying social work. Ironically, my dad was right when he deterred me from it—this path had turned out so much better.

As much as those thoughts inspired me, the first day sitting among the Danish doctors and health professionals, I felt totally out of place and as timid as a mouse. It was ludicrous. How was I supposed to lead them when I didn't know what I was doing there? I kept feeding myself more intimidation tactics. Luckily, John Porting had arranged daily check-in times with me as part of the training. There, he took me to task. "What do you think you are doing, not saying anything?" he frowned at me.

"I, um, am worried that I will say something inappropriate. People will think I shouldn't really be here. I don't know if I have anything to contribute," I replied timidly. He didn't seem too perturbed. "Let's see. Maybe you can start with what you wanted to say. For example, when it came to Thomas. Surely you have some ideas about how he presented?" he asked, smiling encouragingly.

That was easy. I had keenly observed Thomas and saw tremendous anger and self-hatred in this young doctor. Once I started sharing my perceptions and suggestions of what to do I couldn't stop talking.

"These are excellent observations, Elke," he said. "Now, next time you say exactly that. Never mind the others in the room or what they think. They can have a different opinion. But from what you have told me, you are spot on." And with that, our first consultation was done.

The next day I spoke my perceptions and suggestions out loud. It was freeing and well received by the participants. I learned that it was best for me to just to let the inspiration, which never failed to drop in, come out of my mouth. I became a well-respected leader in those three weeks and I never doubted the value of this inspiration again.

The workshop made it possible for me to work for a mental health association in Toronto that dealt with former psychiatric patients. It was ideal for me: I was able to earn money and gain experience working part-time while completing my master's degree. In the mental health association, a psychiatrist invited me to observe while he treated his patients and learn how he diagnosed mental health disorders. I was supposed to teach him group therapy techniques and gestalt methods in return. I was enthusiastic, and at the same time, could not believe how much trust was already placed in me.

This would never happen in Germany, I thought. Nobody would have let me be a part of a session like this without a master's or a doctorate. The people in Toronto gave me the benefit of the doubt, and I was appreciated for what I delivered. I am forever grateful for this.

This realization led to the conclusion that even if I wanted to return to Germany, I could not go back. So many possibilities were open to me in Canada. In addition, returning to Germany would mean I had to translate all the technical terms, methods and scientific approaches again and learn them in German.

Apart from those reasons, I was doing well on a personal level. I was living with three medical students in a residential community. We cooked together, philosophized, debated, argued and laughed until late at night. One of them was my boyfriend for a year. He was a talented musician and finally decided to study medicine. Coincidentally, he was Jewish, and this would have been my chance to introduce someone to my parents in Straubing. But I quickly realized that our relationship was not going to last long.

After completing my Master of Psychology, Dean's List, I began work in a youth clinic. I was doing exactly what I had always wanted to do: helping people make the desired changes in their lives they could not on their own. With my now solid salary, I bought a small car and felt really grown up. I also designed and presented high school seminars for girls to help them develop greater self-esteem. For this, I even received an award from the municipality and a lot of praise from my boss. I earned good money, and sometimes did not know what to spend it on. It was like a dream, but after two years of the same job I was getting restless.

On my way to work one morning, I browsed through a home and lifestyle magazine at a kiosk. That's it, I thought—I will buy a house! This would make me independent from landlords and help me build up a retirement nest egg. I was single and I often thought about what would happen to me when I was old. The idea became clear, and the challenge, too. I had to earn at least twice as much to take out a loan for a house and to have the chance to pay it off. The next logical step for me was to look for a new job.

I learned that a psychological consultant to a business earned more money than working for a clinic and I thought I would enjoy the work even more. Now I had only to find the right people to help me with my plans. I heard this was done through networking, and I started to meet people to ask who might know of a business consulting job using my background. I would be bringing the knowledge from my years in therapy and the experiences I had at home in my parents' shop in Straubing.

I found a company that hired me as a management consultant and personal development consultant to CEOs. The owner of this management consulting company came from a therapy background himself. He applied his family therapy experience to companies, which he viewed like family systems. I had found the right company.

I received a big assignment in which I had to interview all the VPs in a printing company and report my findings to the CEO. I was told by the owner of the consulting company that the CEO was an icon in the printing industry, a formidable man and not easily impressed. I was mortified but pushed through the "Who am I to give him advice?" fear and decided to throw all caution to the wind. I just spoke from the heart and explained how the relationship with his VPs could be improved. I gave him a quick analysis of their behavior, how they were at odds with each other, and how he could restructure things so he would achieve more cohesiveness, as well as profit. His comment—"Frankly, Ms. Michalowicz, I'm impressed"—still caught me by surprise, but this time I had no impulse to turn around to check if he was talking to someone else, as I had with the Oxford professor just a few years earlier.

The little deli apprentice had grown into a woman who could stand toe to toe with the most formidable men. Amongst VPs and CEOs, I often thought of my parents' shop and how they solved problems. Their initiative, people skills and attention to quality control made them successful. If they could do this just intuitively, I was confident I too could impart the most relevant skills to the businesses I was entrusted with. The owner of the management consultant company enthused, "Your credibility in the company is unmatched, your suggestions are being carried out and we are happy to make you senior consultant." I was compensated accordingly, and several months later I had enough money to make a down payment on a house in Toronto.

It was an incredible feeling to walk barefoot over the brand new, cream-colored carpet, to sit on my pastel couch or to cook something in my kitchen. I knew that it was something special to buy a house as a woman alone, and it was great that I had earned everything in it, from the bookshelf to the bedside lamp. When I lay in my new bed on the evening of the move, I felt the tension ebb away. I had accomplished something; now I could be reassured. I had seldom slept as well as that night. But this feeling did not last long. When I looked around my neighborhood, there were a lot of women around my age, all married and with at least two children.

Every morning, as I went to work, the fathers started their cars and the women stood on the porches with their children, waving. In the evening, sitting on my terrace, I watched the little ones play. I loved listening to their laughter and had to laugh myself when one of them said something funny. Of course, I questioned myself: would I ever have children?

For the first time in a long time I was not in a relationship. I had a wonderful home and a well-paying job, and I knew that my parents were very proud of me. I would have liked nothing more than to welcome my parents to Canada and show them everything I had worked for. But my father would never be able to make the trip, no matter how hard he tried.

I had achieved everything I had come to Canada for. But I was alone, without a partner or my immediate family. Should I have stayed in Straubing?

Would I have been happier there? What kind of person would I have been if I had taken over my parents' store and married Daniel, my fiancé? Was it fair for me to leave my parents? Did I do all the leaving of partners out of a fear of abandonment?

I was still feeling it, this vulnerability, this fear of abandonment. It was telling me I would get hurt and never love and feel loved, not fully. Now that I had accomplished everything I'd set out to do, there wasn't a mother, a father, or a partner to hug and share closeness with. I realized, though, that I could manage on my own, and staying single was a possibility. I wasn't going to settle for a relationship that didn't feel right and I didn't know if anybody ever would. It was even more important that at work, I was going strong.

In 1989, the vice president of a firm I was consulting for offered me a permanent job at his company. Over twenty-five hundred employees, most of them engineers, worked there. I liked the idea of having my own office and a regular income. With the management consulting company, each contract was for a certain period of time, and after that I would have to come up with something new to further the operations and employees of a different company. It was exciting and lucrative but also exhausting. New problems had to be solved constantly. In my own office, I could concentrate on one company, and I would not have to constantly prove that I was worth investing in. I accepted the offer.

While my office and position as Manager of the Personnel Development Department was being created, I took a few weeks off and traveled first to Guatemala and then met my friend, Gina, in Lanzarote, one of the Canary Islands. On our third day we were tired of lying on the beach and Gina and I decided to climb one of the dormant volcanic mountains. The sun heated our skin and the black rocks almost seemed to be boiling. The way up was arduous. We climbed over big boulders and had to be careful not to stumble. At the top, we paused and ate and drank the provisions we carried in our backpacks. When my breathing and pulse had returned to normal, I stood up and looked around. We were surrounded by the Atlantic, which lay before of us in shades of blue from delicate turquoise to navy. I breathed deeply of the indescribable air—dry, hot and still salty from the sea.

Suddenly, I felt a tingling. Goose bumps ran down my arms and my heart beat faster. At first, I thought I was experiencing sunstroke, but I wasn't dizzy. On the contrary, everything suddenly seemed clear. And then a voice came through: *You'll meet the man you're going to marry within a month.* I turned around hastily and looked at my girlfriend. Had she just said that? But she just sat on a rock, munching her apple and looking in another direction. I couldn't help but blurt out to her what I had just experienced. I immediately qualified it with a dismissive chuckle. "What does that even mean? No way would I meet somebody within a month let alone marry them."

She laughed along with me. "Ha, ha, you sure this is really water in your bottle?"

Three weeks later, I started my new job at the company in Toronto. First, I had to attend a workshop to get an overview of the people and politics of the company. I sat at a long oval table with about twenty men wearing grey or black pants and striped shirts. Just as the workshop was about to begin, there was a crashing sound at the door. It opened slowly. A man with a cast on his foot came limping in on crutches. He was younger than the others, had short brown hair and wore a red-and-black plaid lumberjack shirt with jeans. He had taken the suggestion to wear casual clothing to the workshop quite seriously. It took a while until he could sit down with his crutches on one of the chairs. He sat directly opposite me and stared. I had watched every move and caught myself thinking that he probably did not have a desk job in the company because he obviously did not think twice about office clothes. Perhaps a construction worker? Otherwise, I could not explain why he was so muscular in contrast to the others. I was distracted and I felt that he was inspecting me too. What was he thinking?

Suddenly, I felt it again: the tingling and the goosebumps I had on the volcano in Lanzarote. My heart raced and I tried to tell myself it was absurd. The man works in the same company as you and is also younger than you! Forget it.

The workshop started and I simply could not concentrate on what was being said. I tried to look at him as inconspicuously as possible, then was startled as our eyes met. What's the matter with him? I thought. Flirting with me at this workshop, this is too ridiculous. I turned away and looked at the man who was speaking.

Now we were supposed to introduce ourselves in turn, and I was very curious about what he would have to say. I liked his voice immediately: "My name is Matt Babicki. I'm a mechanical engineer, and I like to spend my weekends mountain climbing," he said, grinning at me. I think at that moment my heart stopped.

The vice president had given me a list of staff I should be talking to. The name, Matthew Babicki, was at the top of the list. I remembered how much the VP had raved about him and told me that this young man should be supported in his promotion and remain with the company.

A week after I had interviewed Matt personally, he called me and asked if I wanted to go to dinner with him that night. Of course, I wanted to—but I knew the company rule was that you could not date anyone who was dependent on you. And this was the case with Matt's promotion—I had to make an assessment and then a decision on whether I approved of his promotion or not. But since I had already said yes to the promotion and had begun negotiations with his boss, we did not have to worry about a conflict of interest. Matt and I talked about it and came to the conclusion that he would remain in the company whether he got the promotion or whether we went out for dinner or not.

After a few months, it was clear we wanted to marry and spend our lives together. Now I had to go to the VP and confess this to him. I waited for him after an evening meeting with all the managers that had lasted several hours.

"I have to tell you something," I stammered.

"Yes?" he looked up, looking worried.

"I am seeing someone from the company, and we want to get married."

"Oh! And who is it?" he asked.

I told him it was Matt and made him the offer that one of us would leave the company immediately, as we were both aware of the breach of rules. The VP should decide which one of us to keep and which one of us should leave. I talked and talked because I was upset and unsure, and I felt sorry for causing so much confusion.

But he grinned and stopped me. "Matt? That's great! Congratulations! You suit each other well." He reached out his hand to shake mine.

"Um, thank you. But which one of us should stay?" I asked impatiently. Matt and I had talked about it for hours and gone through every possible scenario.

"That is not even up for debate. You will both stay," he boomed, looking at me with a serious expression.

"But isn't there a rule that says …" I could not believe he'd just leave it at that.

"Yeah," he said, laughing. "There is such a rule. I wrote that rule. So, screw the rule."

We got married in 1990 and both stayed with the company over another year when we thought about starting a family. Matt wanted to go back to Vancouver where he grew up and where his parents still lived on the North Shore. He grew up hiking and skiing and loved having the local mountains in his backyard. We would be close to his family when it came time to think of starting our own. He didn't have to try too hard to persuade me. I had been to Vancouver before and knew how beautiful it was.

We packed our belongings, loaded them into a truck and drove more than forty-five hundred kilometers to Vancouver. In the weeks before our move, we talked a lot about having children. Married couples had told us their stories about not being able to conceive. I was worried. I had tried everything over the past few years not to get pregnant, so as not to endanger my career. Maybe it wasn't possible anymore?

While driving past countless lakes, farmhouses and mountains, Matt and I didn't talk about having children. Maybe it would not happen for us; perhaps it was not meant to be. We needed twelve days for our move, and at every rest stop, I had to buy sour gummy bears in all different flavors. One evening I noticed that I had completely emptied an entire bag by myself in only one day. Strange, I thought.

When we arrived in British Columbia in the small town with the meaningful name of Hope, flowers were blooming, and the buds of the trees were blossoming. "Finally, no more ice-cold winters that last an eternity," I said to Matt and laughed.

We watched the sun go down behind the high snow-capped mountains, and Matt said, "Now we can say goodbye to our old life and welcome our new one." In many ways, he was right.

The next day we reached Vancouver and moved into a house on the North Shore a friend of Matt's family had made available to us for a few months. Magnolias blossomed in the front yard, and I felt comfortable from the first moment in this bright, brand-new house.

I stepped over the cartons we were unpacking and headed towards the terrace, where Matt was taking in the stunning view of the city. It was time to join him for a little break. Instead of feeling peaceful when I looked out, I began to feel dizzy. The trees seemed to sway too much. I felt like I was on a ship, seasick. Then I realized what was happening.

I looked at my husband. "Matt, I think I'm pregnant."

Our daughter, Sasha, was born in December 1991. We liked that Sasha is the short form for Alexandra, after my dad's name, Alexander. As a middle name, I wanted to name her Lucia after my mother's grandmother. I never knew her, but my mother had described her so intimately. An ocean separated us, but this was a way to keep them close.

"Hi," I whispered, as I held my daughter for the first time. The bond was so powerful and immediate, it could never be called into question. I felt like a lioness who would do anything to protect her young. It actually connected me closer to my father, who I realized had this intensity of emotion, this protectiveness. It made me understand the sorrow and fear that motivated him to protect me against all possible evils, from nuns and cruel boys. My mom was the supportive rock in my life, but my dad was ready to be the lion roaring with power and fight all my battles.

I could feel both my parents coming through in how I behaved as a mother. I would dance with Sasha in my arms and sing German and Yiddish songs to her. We could not stop looking at each other. She liked being talked to, smiled readily and preferred that I move around rather than sit while I held her in my arms. I liked showing her things, as she was a very inquisitive baby, studying everything with great interest. This perceptiveness and curiosity never changed—every day she found new territory to explore and she grew into a beautiful and independent young lady. She too is not afraid to stand toe to toe with formidable men or women.

Loving and protecting my child is like breathing air. I have recorded her first words, photographed special moments and made a memory book for her, every year. Sasha is the greatest miracle that has ever happened to me.

Of course, I also had low points. Being a mother was the most difficult and energy-sapping thing I had ever experienced. And yet, there was nothing more rewarding. I also admit that I had my moments in which I would have loved to exchange my life for that of a single woman. But when Sasha babbled "Mama" and smiled at me, everything else was forgotten.

Later, in Sasha's teen years, I embarrassed her. When I once again turned the Stones up and danced through the house, she stood motionless, raised her eyebrows, looked at me skeptically and said, "Seriously, now?"

I was most sorry that Sasha did not want to pursue singing when she was a teenager, even though she had a strikingly beautiful voice. One of her singing teachers once asked me who she had most likely inherited her talent from in her family. "From my father," I replied, without hesitating for a second.

Even though Sasha sometimes rolled her eyes when we said something, I knew exactly how much she appreciated her parents. Just as my parents did, Matt and I took turns driving her to a private school and picking her up again. We kept up this daily ritual for many years, and though it was an effort, we also learned a lot about each other in this small, confined space.

Having a child is a long journey. In essence, from their first second in the world, you are preparing your child to be able to leave you and lead an independent life. The tiny, cute baby you held in your arms will hold hands with boys, drive a car herself and clearly express her own opinions. Today, the most important thing for me is to keep our special mother–daughter bond intact, and to enjoy it. In the close connection with my baby I know one thing for sure: I've never loved anyone more than her.

What tremendous strength it must have taken for my parents to let me go. Their love found it possible to support my coming to Canada to fulfill my calling. They became my cheerleaders despite their sadness of being separated from their only child. The massive destruction Hitler's actions created will continue to defy understanding for generations to come. His calculated cruel plot brought my parents so much grief and heartache. And yet, their true essence was indestructible. The war that should have kept them apart had brought them together. They walked hand in hand for more than fifty-five years.

Sasha would be able to get to know her grandparents in Vancouver well, but what chance would she have to get to know my parents? I introduced Sasha to my parents when she was less than a year old. We made sure to visit for a few weeks at the very least every second year. But sadly, with the distance, my parents not speaking English and not being able to travel, it was never enough for them to really get to know each other.

Instead of dwelling on regret for what could have been, I focused on being grateful for the strength my parents had provided to create this new life in Canada. The mystery to solve was not what could have been, but what I had become as a result of all that.

Eighteen months after Sasha's birth, I started working as an independent employee consultant for companies. In my own practice in the Ambleside district of West Vancouver, I spoke with employees to make them feel better in their lives and to ultimately perform better for their business. I worked with a mixture of methods to deal with stress, tension, depression, trauma, phobias and conflicts in relationships.

In 2004, something happened during a treatment that immediately reminded me of the bicycle accident and the thirty-four dollars and thirty-eight cents. I was at my desk when there came a knock at the door. I knew the next client was a social worker who had received funding for therapy from her employer. Slowly the door opened, and a woman peered in and greeted me with a smile. She was Indo-Canadian, with long, black, shiny hair, honey-colored skin and dark brown eyes. She looked around my treatment room. It was important to me to set it up to feel more like a living room in a home. Fluffy carpet, comfortable armchairs, flowers, indirect light and paintings that show scenes from Italy, one my favorite countries.

"I'm here for grief counselling," said the woman and sat down on the couch. I noticed that she was not used to talking about herself—that usually she listened to others. She told me her younger brother had died in a car accident at only twenty-six.

Since this was my first meeting with her, I asked her about her family and their story, which is how I try to build trust with my clients. After the meeting, we agreed on a next appointment. My day went on as usual. I had consultations with other clients and in the evening, I ate with Matt and Sasha on our terrace. Just before falling asleep, I thought about the woman again. I could see her face—which had appealed to me so much—right in front of me. How terrible it was to lose a brother through an accident.

In the middle of the night, I woke up with a start, my heart throbbing, sweat running down my neck. I sat bolt upright. Matt lay next to me breathing quietly; he did not wake up easily. I gasped for air. A voice had woken me up, whispering in my ear: *This was an intercultural, interracial hate crime.* I was still half asleep, but everything seemed to be happening quite vividly—just as in Lanzarote on the volcano. Even so, I turned to Matt. But it could not have been him speaking, I could hear him snoring. Had the young man really died in a car accident? How in the world can you have such crazy dreams? I asked myself. I didn't know what to do—what did this sentence mean?

The next morning, I was still upset, my hands trembling. I tried to organize my thoughts. The young woman said he died in an accident. Period! But where did this dream come from?

Like when I had the dream that announced the exact price of the repair after my bike accident, I finally came to the realization that there seemed to be something happening outside of the reality we live in every day. What kind of voice was it? Did it come from another world? Was it a wiser part of me? Could it even have been the dead brother who wanted to tell me something? Icy chills ran down my spine. It was uncanny. It was imperative that I tell my client at our next meeting.

A week later, I saw the young woman again. I explained to her that I had dreamed something, but it was possible that it was silly and might have nothing to do with her and her family at all. I also confessed to her that the dream had occupied my thoughts for days.

When I told her about the dream, she stared at me with her mouth open. Her eyes filled with tears. She blew her nose in a handkerchief and began shaking her head.

"No, no …" she murmured. "No, it is not possible," she said at last. "I can't believe it. Where did you hear this?"

Now it burst out of her: There was indeed serious racial unrest and abductions in Trinidad, and her brother had been found dead in his car. The family believed he had tried to escape his persecutors. There were, however, no witnesses who could have said anything about the accident. The family desperately tried to figure out what had happened to him. They failed, however, because of the corrupt authorities, and had not learned anything yet.

"We have no chance at all to find out anything," she said, and began to cry, "but what you have just told me is like a message from my brother."

"Well, I don't know," I answered skeptically. "I'm not so sure."

In the next sessions she brought her family with her. We talked about my observations, dreams and emotions about this young man who had loved his family so much and who was now deeply missed by them. I had the impression they were very relieved to be talking about it.

My Master's graduation, a proud day!

*During the time I was working at the youth clinic,
this is me having fun dancing.*

Here Matt and I are on the way to a formal function at Sasha's school.

Here is my daughter Sasha at five years old with me at the Ambleside beach in West-Vancouver.

Sasha at 14 years old on one of our Europe trips

Matt and me in the Lighthouse park area in West Vancouver in 2011

Chapter 14

Adapt and live

In 2005 a year after the dream of the death of the young man, I was again startled in the middle of the night by a vivid dream. My father had a problem with his leg—it became paralyzed, and although everything seemed to be all right, he collapsed and died a short time later. The thought of this dream now haunted me every day.

Perhaps that's why it did not surprise me when my mother called a year later and told me that, while taking a walk, my father suddenly could not move one of his legs. Luckily, they were close to home, and when they arrived, he collapsed.

We had just moved to our new home near Lighthouse Park in West Vancouver. Boxes were everywhere and a continuous stream of construction workers and painters were in and out of the house. I listened to my mother on the telephone while looking out to the Pacific Ocean from our terrace. "Mama, I'm going to take the next plane to Munich. I do not like the sound of this."

"Oh, no, that is not necessary. Elke, you don't have to come such a long way. He'll get better. Your father squeezed my hand today and said he'll see me again tomorrow." She tried to calm me down, and for a short time I thought she was probably right. But there was something in me that said just the opposite: You have to go home. Your father is going to die.

Though my dad didn't yodel like my grandfather just before he passed, something else remarkable happened. After he collapsed, he had been going in and out of consciousness and was being tested by various doctors to determine what was really happening with him. One of the doctors was a neurologist. He was showing my father various objects and asking him questions, but my dad remained unconscious and unable to respond. My mom told me on the phone that things looked very dire, but when the doctor asked, "Herr Michalowicz, do you have children?" suddenly Dad awoke from his fugue state and said, "Yes, I have a daughter, and she is a psychologist in Canada." The neurologist was still baffled at how this could be, but my mom thought it meant he was getting better and it was not necessary for me to get on the plane to Germany.

Had I not had the dream that predicted my dad would not survive, I probably would have listened to her. As it was, I knew it meant something different would happen and I needed to be on my way to my parents.

Thanks to the dream I was able to get there just in time to hold my father's hand while he was preparing to leave this earth. My mother whispered words of endearment to make him stay, but I felt he needed encouragement to have the strength to go. This was another very difficult ocean for him to cross—he was struck by a fear similar to being forced to cross the first bottomless ocean, which was filled with monsters when he was just fifteen. I kept telling him, "You can do this, Dad. You have done so well in everything, you are an amazing guy and I love you. You can do this. You are brave and it will be okay." His lurching death rattle continued but over time his breathing spasms grew quieter until there was no sound at all. Six hours after I arrived, Dad passed, looking serene and peaceful. I whispered, "I'm here, don't you worry. I'll help Tilly get through this." At that moment I experienced my dad's presence more profoundly than the years before when he was aging. There was a feeling of peace, softness and light in the room and my dad looked younger and more serene than I'd seen him in many years. I was in awe. My dad was at peace.

Eight years later I dreamed about my mother. She stood at my bedside in West Vancouver, gave me a kiss on the cheek and whispered in my ear, "Elke, you are my one and everything, never forget that." I felt her warmth, her love and her lips on my skin. I felt just like that little girl who had waited for her to finally have time for me and be able to read me a story.

The next morning, someone from St. Nikola's Seniors' Home in Straubing called me in Canada. My mother had passed during the night. On April 26, 2014, Matt and I flew to Germany for her funeral at the Jewish cemetery in Straubing. When I held the plane ticket in my hands, I saw it in black and white. Exactly eight years ago, on April 26, 2006, the same hour, I had also been sitting in a plane to visit my father in the hospital in Straubing a few hours before he died. My mother would have had a chuckle. She always pointed out those kind of numbers to me and said, "That's no coincidence; they send a message."

She was the one who pointed out the number of her room in the seniors' home when we moved her into it. Her name was listed at the door beside the room number, 2246, a number that contained the date of Matt's and my birthdays—we were both born in June, he on the 4th and I on the 22nd. Mom always thought 22 was her lucky number anyhow, and she said, "Now, every time I enter the room I feel protected."

Mom was active in the seniors' home, loved by many, and the staff came to tell her the stories of their lives. She was surrounded with protection and felt lucky that way. Mom also died the way she lived, she got it done without fuss and I know she didn't want to experience the pain of saying goodbye to me. I was amazed that distance didn't matter, as Mom came to me in a dream anyhow. When I spoke to the kind nurse to find out what happened, she told me that Mom felt unwell, called for help and had the nurse and a doctor by her side over the next fifteen minutes. They held her hand while she struggled with her last breath. There is so much we can't explain, but really there was no denying it. I felt my mom's presence more keenly than ever. She too was at peace.

Four months later, Matt and I traveled to Munich again to meet up with my childhood friend Hanjo and his wife, Martina. From Munich we flew to Johannesburg to go on a safari. Safari is the Swahili word for "travel" or "expedition." We had planned and booked this trip months before my mother passed away. After my father's death, both my mother and I cherished the lengthy phone conversations we had twice a week. Her mind was as sharp as ever, she was a great listener and she gave good advice. We could talk about anything with each other. We also spoke about this Africa trip and the animals we would see. When we were on the safari, I felt my mom's presence as if she was there enjoying every moment with me. It became the journey of our lives, a journey that brought the past and the future together as one.

As we crossed the Mediterranean, I imagined how Grandfather Johann had come to Africa during the Second World War to fight in Rommel's Afrika Korps, and I realized how terrible it must have been for him to lie wounded and so far from home in a military hospital. From Johannesburg we drove to Victoria Falls in what is Zimbabwe today. Near the falls, we ate African barbecue, danced to the rhythm of drums and felt a bit like Zulu warriors. This is when I remembered standing on the stage as a four-year-old at the Mariandl in Straubing and moving to the rhythm of the music. Dancing has followed me all my life. Even as a child, I wanted to take ballet lessons. Later I taught aerobics classes and to this day, I enjoy going to dance lessons and letting off steam in a club in the evenings.

Our next stop was the Chobe Game Lodge in northern Botswana. We floated along the Chobe River in a boat, watching elephant herds playing in the water a few meters away and photographed hippos and crocodiles relaxing in the sun.

The next day we drove in an open jeep with a guide through the steppes to see lions. It was early in the morning, the ideal time to see the predators of the night find their way to their sleeping places. In the steppes it was still chilly, so we were glad to have warm jackets and hats to protect us from the wind in the open jeep. It would be hotter in a few hours.

"The lions should be no problem to find; we are constantly coming across them," the guide said. "But if you're really lucky, we may discover a leopard."

The woman told us how shy leopards are and that they usually hunt only at night and hide in the trees during the day. We nodded and hoped that we would be able to marvel at and photograph a lion at least.

Suddenly our guide flinched and hissed, "Hold on tight. I'll turn off the road here into the bush and drive quickly." She whispered, "I think I saw a leopard," and stepped on the accelerator. "You're so lucky! I'm going to cut him off." She veered off the main road and continued to hit the gas, the engine roaring. The jeep shook and jolted as we drove over tree trunks and through huge potholes. I worked hard not to fall out, holding on with all my might. Then we stopped.

Our guide said quietly, "You can now stand up and see the leopard. But please move very slowly. He seems to be approaching us."

Standing at the back exit to the jeep, I had an unobstructed view and was fascinated as the leopard moved silently and gracefully over the steppes with his impressive paws. His spotted fur shone in the sun. With every movement, we could see its muscles rippling under its skin.

Everyone in the jeep was silent. I could hear the breathing of the others, the wind blowing past us, and the chirping of crickets. I stood on the top step of the small step ladder of the jeep and suddenly noticed that the leopard was not only coming toward us but seemed to be looking at me. Since the jeep was open, I had absolutely no protection. The first thing on my mind was what I could do with my camera now that I was so close. Would the movement of my hands and the clicking disturb him? Did I dare? I pressed the shutter button. The next thought: Did the leopard see me as a single living entity there on top of the step ladder? Or did I seem part of the jeep in my camouflage clothes? The leopard moved silently toward me and stopped at the lowest step of the ladder. I stood on the highest. Our eyes met. His eyes looked almost like that of a person: black pupils and a delicate, translucent green around it.

At that moment, the world stopped. I felt I did not need to be afraid—it would have been too late anyway. If he jumps up and attacks me, I thought, I would be seeing my parents again very soon. This idea comforted me and I did not panic. A few seconds later, the leopard turned a little to the side and changed direction, probably to pass the jeep. He brushed up against the bumper with his furry coat and trotted quietly, as if in slow motion, away from us. We stared after him until we saw him climb a tree and disappear. We sat down again, and I saw from the faces of the others that they were just as shaken by what had happened as I was.

The guide said, "In the wild, there are only three possibilities—you move on, you adapt, or you die. The leopards here are chased by lions who hunt in prides. Perhaps the leopards are so hard to hunt because they have the ability to hide and be silent." She pointed towards the steppe. "Leopards are loners. But their advantage is that they are incredibly fast and that they can outwit lions." She laughed, the others nodded enthusiastically, and I thought of my father. I understood how he survived the concentration camps and created a whole new life afterward.

From Chobe, we flew in a small Cessna into the middle of the Okavango Delta to the wilderness camp Kwetsani.

The only method of transportation was those small aircraft. Once there, our new guide, who had grown up in the Okavango Delta, greeted us. With him, we climbed into a shaky aluminum boat and he raced it along the waterways the hippos had created. I felt like I was on a roller coaster ride, but there were no rails here and no seat belts. The reeds brushed up against the boat, water sprayed up, and we tried not to fall out.

Over the next days we glided in the elongated Mokoro boats through the waterways. The boats were about four meters long and once were cut from a single tree. Now they are made of fiberglass. Our guide in the stern ferried the boat along the narrow waterways with a long pole. He was an expert at not coming too close to the enormous animals. We watched as the hippos raised their eyes above the water and how they twirled their little ears. Hippos can open their mouths extremely wide, and we were especially glad our guide was so experienced.

Overnight we stayed in treehouses, accessible by wooden walkways built like bridges. As usual, Matt immediately fell asleep, while I was still thinking about the day. The walls of our treehouse were made of thin planks and I could hear every cricket, every bird, and the wind in the leaves of the trees. I found it very soothing. Faded moonlight shone through the glass doors leading to the terrace and the mosquito netting across our bed moved gently in the wind. I closed my eyes.

Shortly before I fell asleep, I suddenly heard the shrill screaming of monkeys and a loud clanking. The monkeys seemed to be jumping from branch to branch over our tree house and were completely beside themselves. Branches whipped down on the roof of our house. When I already thought that it was unbearably loud, something drowned out the hysterical shrieking, something that could only be one thing—the roar of a lion who had just slain its prey. It sounded so close that I first thought he was standing in front of our tree house. Now even Matt had woken up. Was this all happening in front of our fragile glass door? Now the monkeys screamed even louder. My heart pounded and when I saw Matt's face, I was even more frightened. When he is scared, you know it's bad.

"Should we put a table in front of the door?" I whispered hesitantly, knowing the answer.

"No, we just have to wait, now," Matt whispered. I could tell by his voice that he was as nervous as I was.

The monkeys shrieked, rattled and crashed. Furniture on the terrace was being knocked over. I briefly considered whether we should set off our previously agreed-on alarm to the manager of the lodge, in case something happened. But what would that do? We had to stay calm and wait until the noise was over.

There in the treehouse, huddled in bed, I thought back to my father. Who are you, when everything is torn away, and you are left without protection? Everything can rapidly go in the wrong direction, whether you are facing a lion from the steppes or the Third Reich.

But my father adapted to the conditions in the camps, fought his way through and never gave up. These are the rules of survival. Because he had fought his way through Ganacker to Straubing, he met my mother and I came into the world. I also experienced a lot and had to go through a few things—but I would not be the person I am now had it all not happened.

The next day, when it got light at about six o'clock, we dared to venture out. A few chairs lay scattered on the terrace, but it was quiet and peaceful now and the first rays of sunshine shone in our faces. We met with Hanjo and his wife at breakfast on the large camp terrace, where we ate fresh fruit and talked about what we had heard in the night. Our guide explained that a lioness, who housed her young close by, had gone on an antelope hunt during the night.

I looked out over the grasslands and realized that Africa had changed something in me. The simplest things in nature, totally primitive and instinctive, can explain so many complicated things. Here, in the wild, everything was still in its original form. Everything is all about one thing: survival. On the safari one thing played out in constant motion—move, adapt or die. This truly was the philosophy my parents lived by.

Epilogue

Matt and I sit on our balcony, savoring our breakfast. We can see Vancouver Island to the west and the Lionsgate Bridge to the east. The sun shines and we breathe in the fresh, salty sea air. My husband came back from a business trip a few days ago, and on the plane he saw the movie *Bicycle Thief*, an Italian black-and-white classic from 1948. The film takes place in the post-war period in Rome and is about a poor family. The father's bike that he so desperately needs for his work is stolen. To keep his family above water, the father tries to get the bike back.

"It was as a movie should be, honest and genuine," said Matt. "It's really a pity that no one makes such movies today, or even write such books anymore." Matt is like that. He can't stand corny love stories and elaborate action films. He wants to be told authentic stories, wants to observe people, to see their development and understand what has influenced them. I agree with him. It was clear from the beginning that this book must be written in such a way.

The answers to many questions lie within us. I believe that life comes together like a big poster-board picture with various puzzle pieces, bit by bit, past and future, making the whole. For the most part, one does not see the complete picture, but only a small puzzle piece of the big Life Poster. But sometimes, very rarely, there are moments when we recognize how it all comes together and everything makes sense. That's when we are connected to the Greater Whole.

I experienced one of those moments of serendipity relating to Steven Spielberg when I visited my cousins, Sollie and Esther, in eastern Canada. We sat in front of the TV and watched a documentary that director Steven Spielberg had made with survivors of the Holocaust while filming *Schindler's List.*

One of the people interviewed was Uncle Henjek, Aunt Hanna's husband. I tried to scribble as many notes as possible during the show, producing several pages of a barely legible scrawl.

But that did not matter. In those few minutes, around seventy years after the end of the Second World War, it became clear how much we and our parents were shaped by these events. Henjek's description of the various camps to which he had been transported, and what he discovered there, hit us hard.

Everyone who has seen the 1993 movie *Schindler's List* remembers the scenes in which the Nazi criminal, Amon Göth, indiscriminately shoots people from his balcony in the Plaszow concentration camp.

When the documentary was over, my cousins and I cried and held each other's hands.

Things could have been so different: my father could have stayed close to his sister for the rest of his life. But because of the Holocaust, the time they spent together was far too short.

The other side of this tragedy is that it led me to be who I am, and to move somewhere "across the ocean" to Canada, as my great-grandmother, Lucia, had predicted. If my dad had not been such a fighter, he would never have survived, and if I had not fought him the way I did as a teenager, I would not be where I am now.

Over the past forty years, I've expended a lot of energy to reclaim power over my life. Much had already been mapped out, and the way was paved, but my decision to go to Canada changed something in me. I designed my own life, made my own decisions, and embarked on a great voyage, rather than just letting things happen.

After breakfast I go for my usual walk along the seawall to Ambleside Park. The ocean crashes and seagulls screech. I think about a visit to close friends, Jim and Andrea. As we watched them cook dinner, Andrea asked me about the memoir. She wanted to know everything about my father, especially about when he hid under the corpses in Ganacker. It was strange to talk about it and watch her cut fresh vegetables.

But my friend did not let herself be distracted and said, "So, he felt like he had to set out to escape this hell. He was one step ahead of them, and that helped him survive." She sipped her glass of wine. "I think he simply trusted his instinct. But Elke, he must have been a fighter, or he could not have endured something like that."

Jim nodded, "There are certainly not many who could have done it," he cleared his throat. "Honestly, I do not know what kind of strength one must have to do this."

Andrea added, "The intuition to be able to interpret a situation like this correctly is something special." She winked at me and lifted her glass of wine. "Cheers! Here's to intuition! I am very glad your father listened to his—otherwise, you would not be sitting here today."

We clinked glasses and laughed. We went out into their garden again. The last rays of the sun shone orange over the Pacific. I admired the flowers in my friends' garden and sat down on a comfortable, cushioned chair. I closed my eyes. The sun, though almost gone, warmed my face. I thought how my parents would have enjoyed this peace, the tulips and the chirping birds. Inwardly, I sent them a message. You are a significant part of me, and I am convinced that you are happy to see me like this!

My parents among the poppies

Acknowledgments

When you are writing a book, many people are involved before you have the privilege of connecting with your readers. My appreciation for all the people who have contributed to creating this book is almost impossible to put into words. I would like to express my immense gratitude to the following:

Susanne Martin, fluent in both English and German, who was the first to edit my English translation from the German version.

Many thanks to Geoff Armstrong who called from New York to tell me the manuscript moved him so much that it kept him awake. He helped guide this project with great insight and enthusiasm.

My gratitude goes to Jennifer Williams who found my story inspiring and kept encouraging me from her editing office in New York.

My thanks to Sylvia Taylor, Lori Bamber and Betsy Goolsby, who were exacting copyeditors and a delightful team support.

My appreciation goes to Megan Williams, a successful author and founder of an agency for publishing, TSPA. Her smart input had a powerful impact on the transformation from the German to the English version. Thank you Kristy Hill, Anna Mullens, Kirsten Southcott, Jason and Tage for your expertise and help in empowering me to stand on my own intelligence to publish this book.

Many thanks to my wonderful German editor, Sophie Schattenkirchner, for her zest and support in publishing my life story first in Germany. I am eternally grateful to her for the friendship that flourished through our collaboration. Thank you Rosie Moore for coming all the way from Canada to the Straubing book launch, that made it extra special.

I would like to thank Claudia Karl-Fischer, the Head of the Marketing Department of the *Straubing Daily News*. I thank Archivist Dr. Dorit-Maria Krenn, for her scientific references; Hans Vicari, for his insights into life in Straubing at the time of the Second World War; and Hanna Zisler, from the Jewish community center in Straubing, which enabled us to turn them into a part of our story.

Back when my first manuscript was being drafted, many people were involved in offering feedback and helped to improve the book. I would like to thank Cea Person, author of *North of Normal*. In her course I learned how to write the story of my family as if they were living it in the present. This also applies to Richard Boyer, the leader of another writers' group I attended, who encouraged me to believe in my writing style.

My appreciation goes to Karen Hoffman, who motivated me to think of publishing this book first in German, to Cheryl Noble and Carol Sill, who also read my manuscript and supported me in the earlier phases.

When you write your life story, it always means thanking the people who are part of your life. There are not enough pages to express my gratitude.

Thanks to Matt, my incredible husband, who has always encouraged me to pursue what seems to be the most challenging to achieve, and to my wonderful daughter, Sasha, who has given my life more meaning and enriched it more than I ever thought possible. I would also like to mention my Uncle Hans and Uncle Erwin, along with their families—in my heart I am always connected to you, even if I live thousands of miles away. I thank you for your interest and your positive reactions to this book. Above all, I am grateful for how you bravely transported yourself back in time to the Second World War and shared stories from that era.

I would like to thank Cousin Sollie and Cousin Esther. Sollie, without you, I would never have come to Toronto to study. I would like to thank both of you for the great time we spent together in 2016, during which we researched many facts from our mutual past. This enabled me to write the family stories as truthfully as possible. When I think of the interview with your father, Henjek, I would like to thank you again for your emotional support.

Thanks to all my friends on both continents. I am happy that I have found you. You mean the world to me. Thank you for being there along the way. I could not imagine my life without you. With you I have grown and you have made me what I am now.

I would like to express my gratitude to the bright friends in my women's groups, with whom I read and discuss books every month. I truly cherish your insights, curious minds and caring hearts. And many thanks to the women in my fitness group. Your zest for life and go-for-it attitudes inspire me continuously. Thank you for your enthusiastic support and interest in "When will I be able to read it in English?"

Last, but not least, I would like to thank all the people in Straubing who knew and loved my parents and who cared so lovingly for my mother after my father died. The friends, nurses and doctors gave stability to both my parents and then to my mother, to the end.

I carry all of you in my heart. You are a part of this story, and without you it would not have turned out this way.

About the Author

Elke Babicki, M.Ed., R.C.C. has been a consultant to corporations and a clinical counsellor in private practice in Toronto and Vancouver, Canada for over thirty years. She has led workshops and sessions in Europe and Canada to help thousands of people claim more power in their lives.

Elke was recognized in 2011 with the Women of Worth Leader of the Year Award for her work in supporting and inspiring women across the globe.

She lives with her husband, Matt, an engineer and inventor, by the ocean in West Vancouver, British Columbia.

Identity was published in Germany as *Uebern Ozean* in 2017 with great success.

www.elkebabicki.com

THE UNITED STATES OF AMERICA
VISA
TORONTO
B-2 28 JUL 1977
MULTIPLE
Elke Michalowicz
Nr.C 5648389
Nr.C 5648389
Der Schüler / Die Schülerin
Elke Michalo
Wohnort
Straubing
besucht die/das
(Siegel)
Straubing
über 12
THE REPUBLIC OF ZIMBABWE VISA
SINGLE ENTRY
ZW 028953
IMMIGRATION
MAY 27 2012
JAN 12 2015
31 AUG 2014